LEOPOLD BLOOM
A Biography

by the same author
The Heart Grown Brutal
Jules Verne
The Magic Zoo
James Joyce

PETER COSTELLO

LEOPOLD BLOOM
A BIOGRAPHY

GILL AND MACMILLAN

First published 1981 by
Gill and Macmillan Ltd
Goldenbridge
Dublin 8
with associated companies in
London, New York, Delhi, Hong Kong,
Johannesburg, Lagos, Melbourne,
Singapore, Tokyo

0 7171 1100 8

Origination by Lagamage Company Ltd. Dublin
Printed and bound in Great Britain by
Redwood Burn Ltd., Trowbridge, Wiltshire.

For
Mary's Patrick
21 May 1980

If it is permissible to reconstruct biography on the basis of the known proclivities of one's hero ...

Richard D. Altick: *The Scholar Adventurers*

One, of those, my lord. A plagiarist. A soapy sneak masquerading as a literateur. It's perfectly obvious that with the most inherent baseness he has cribbed some of my best-selling books, really gorgeous stuff, a perfect gem, the love passages in which are beneath suspicion.

Ulysses

... In respect of the recurrent emergence of the theme of sex in the minds of his characters, it must always be remembered that his locale was Celtic and his season spring.

Judge John M. Woolsey

... [He] was many things, but he was certainly the last forty volumes of *Thom's Directory* thinking aloud.

C.P. Curran

Contents

Acknowledgments

The author and publisher wish to thank the Society of Authors, as representatives of the James Joyce estate, for their courtesy in allowing us to make use of *Ulysses* in the writing of this book.

Acknowledgment is due to the Bodley Head Ltd for permission to quote from *Ulysses* by James Joyce.

Thanks are also due to the contemporary advertisers in Thom's *Post Office Directory for Dublin*, whose contribution to this book has been unique and expressive.

... Finiche! Only a fadograph of a yestern scene

After the accident, when his landlady was cleaning out Mr Bloom's bedsitting room, packing his clothes and meagre mementoes, she found in the drawer of the dressing table a large bundle of photographs tied around with green tape.

These, she thought, had better be packed up separately, as his daughter would want to take particular care of what might well be long treasured heirlooms. So, one by one, she dusted them off and packed them neatly into an old shoe box. As she did she looked at each one, trying to puzzle out what it could have held of significance to her lodger.

One of them, a cabinet photograph from Chancellor's, was obviously of Mr Bloom himself with his new wife. On the back was the date: October 1888. So long ago, Mrs Quinn thought, cozy in the warmth of 1937.

Then there was a picture of a stout gentleman, perhaps his father, and on his knee a small girl in a flouncy dress of the 1890s. And another of a schoolboy in a dark blazer and cap lying stretched out along a brick wall at his ease. Was that his son? Surely not, she thought. His son had died at birth, hadn't he said? A snapshot, now with no date to mark its history: it could be anyone at all.

And here was a portrait photo, with the elegant flourish of Lafayette underneath, clearly taken with extra care at greater cost, in which she recognised the woman in the wedding photo, though the pose was more like that of a Gibson girl than a respectable matron. At the bottom of the pile a snap from a family Brownie box camera of a baby girl on a rug kicking her legs. With it was another schoolboy, of more recent date, again in cap and blazer; Belvedere, she thought from the crest on the cap: his grandson?

1

Underneath them all was a wooden case, which opened out to reveal the mirrored surface of an ancient daguerreotype. Held at an angle to the light, the photograph showed up the heavy features of a middle European face. A name on the paper tape was stuck underneath, a strange name, Hungarian she realised, for the name of the country followed. *Szombathely*. Some bath Ellie indeed.

In an envelope were two brown press cuttings, little crumples of black print. *Corporal punishment in girls' schools,* one was headed. And an advertisement, *I Rudolf Virag . . .* A nun in peculiar pose: quite disgusting. She would never have thought it of nice Mr Bloom. There would be no need to keep those, she thought, tossing the envelope to the back of the bright coals in the fireplace, where the edges turned brown, then black, eating across the prurient prints, until they vanished in a fierce flash of flame. There was something else in the envelope. She opened it and shook it out: a small charm for a fob watch chain, decorated with a compass and set square. This was a device unfamiliar to Mrs Quinn. Back it went.

Into the shoe box the photos went, along with Mrs Quinn's speculations. By temperament she was not given to brooding over past experiences. Today was enough for her, thank God. The fragments of past lives and scattered memories did not interest her. But she did hold by family loyalty, so she was surprised that the box was left behind when Mr Bloom's son-in-law called for the things. Perhaps he had thought it was only rubbish, even though she had written PHOTOS on it in blue crayon.

She took to wearing the charm on her special occasion bracelet, until one evening at the Licensed Vintners' Ball at the Ormond, her friend Briget O'Flaherty leant over the table and took up her wrist to look more closely at it.

'Mother of God, Kathleen, you can't wear that.'

'Why not?', asked Mrs Quinn. 'I had it from Mr Bloom who used to lodge with me.'

Only a little lie, she thought.

'But that's a Masonic seal! You can't wear a heathen thing like that.'

The next day the charm was back in the box marked PHOTOS.

Mrs Quinn kept them nevertheless, and after her, her son, thinking that some day they might prove of some value to someone, even if it were only in piecing together those fragments and memories. But she doubted this. To her there had seemed to be nothing exceptional about Mr Bloom. Who would ever again be bothered about him?

1866

Writing Slates. Humphrey Roberts, Bangor, North Wales, Manufacturers of Writing Slates. Hard Wood Frames of the Best Quality. Established 1828.

Peruvian Government Guano. Depôts are established at Dublin, Waterford, Cork, Galway, Sligo, Londonderry and Belfast, where a constant supply is always at hand. Apply to Robert F. Gladstone, Trinity Chambers, 41 Dame-street, Dublin.

Bradford's Patent Washing Machine. Dublin International Exhibition, 1865, Prize Medal. The only one awarded to a Washing Machine.

By Special Appointment, Ironmonger to his Excellency Lord Wodehouse, Lord Lieutenant of Ireland. J. Edmundson & Co., 3 Capel-street.

E. Lawrence and Co., General Brush, Comb, and Perfumery Warehouse, 7 Upper Sackville Street. N.B. The best London, Wax, Sperm, Imperial, Botanic, Composite, and every other description of CANDLES now selling at the smallest remunerative profit.

Robert E. Grady, Coach Builder, 38 Dawson Street, (opposite the Mansion House Gardens), Dublin. Carriages bought and sold on Commission. Carriages to let, with Option of Purchase. Repairs, Painting, Etc., on moderate terms.

Pianofortes and Harmoniums By All the Great London

Makers, For Sale or Hire, On Most Moderate Terms, at Piggott's, 112 Grafton St., Dublin.

The chief vendors sell the reviving FLUID CAMPHOR *of Sir James Murray, so superior to Camphor in substance. This drink is agreeable to the spirits. In low fevers it is restorative; and by the magnesia dissolved in it, Heart-burn, and Uric Acid are prevented—Per oz., 3 grs.*

Every laundress should use Cooney's first-class Indigo Blue. Charles Cooney & Co., Manufacturers of Laundry Blues of every description. Starch and Blacking. Manufactory: Back Lane, Dublin.

George Berg, Professor of Baunscheidtism, 98, Stephen's Green, South, Dublin. — Baunscheidtism *is the new exanthematic healing method, which has derived its name from the inventor, Charles Baunscheidt. It effects not only a perfect cure in most all acute cases, as* Toothache, Earache, Headache, *all Fever Cases, etc., etc., rather in such chronic diseases which have been called incurable, viz. —* Rheumatism, Gout, Nervousness, *and most all* Eye Diseases, *without touching the Eyes, if not is operated on them. Testimonials from Patients of this City can be seen by G. Berg, and he will refer to his patients. If any professional man is inclined to adopt this method the undersigned Baunscheidtist will find himself honoured to assist him, and give instruction without making any charge. He is from the Inventor pointed out as Sole Agent for Ireland to sell his real remedy. Also Lebensweker, Oleum Baunscheidti, and Books for Instruction.*

Surgeon L'Estrange's Patent Trusses, for the Radical Cure of Hernia or Rupture. William Duff, 37 Molesworth Street, Dublin. Truss and Bandage Maker.

Consumption, Coughs, Colds, Asthma, Bronchitis, Neuralgia, Rheumatism, Spasms, Etc. Dr. J. Collis Browne's CHLORODYNE.

Trevor, Margaret (Widow) and Son, (of the Late Hugh Trevor), Plumbers, and Water-Closet Manufacturers, and Gas Fitters, 14 South Anne-street, Dublin.

Personal Elegant Requisites. Under the Patronage of Royalty and the Aristocracy of Europe. Rowland's Macassar Oil. This elegant and fragrant oil possesses extraordinary properties for promoting the growth, restoring, improving, and beautifying Human Hair. Price 3s.6d.; 7s.; 10s.6d., (equal to four small); and 21s. per Bottle.

1

Childhood and Youth

Leopold Bloom was born at six in the morning of 6 May 1866, at 52 Clanbrassil Street in the city of Dublin, in the kingdom of Ireland.

As his ancestors were Jews and his father Hungarian, this event was the almost miraculous outcome of years of wanderings and exile, days of bliss, and the momentary union of distinctive genes.

Few Victorian Dubliners can have boasted such a peculiar lineage. His great-grandfather, a man of the eighteenth century, had actually seen in the flesh the Empress Maria Theresa (1717-1780), riding with her daughter Marie Antoinette.

Their family name was Virag, meaning flower, blossom, or bloom. Among the surviving heirlooms (aside from memories) which Bloom inherited from his father, Rudolph Virag, was a soiled daguerreotype of Rudolph and *his* father, Leopold Virag. This was taken in the studio of their cousin, Stefan Virag of Szesfehervar in Hungary. Rudolph Virag's actual home town was Szombathely, where he was born in 1815. The picture was made as a memento when Rudolph left his native land at the age of thirty-six in 1852.

The country had been thrown into turmoil in the revolution four years before, one of those numerous risings all across Europe in 1848, the year of the *Communist Manifesto*. In Hungary the Jews were not conscious of being in chains. Though anti-semitism was rife in Central Europe, it was uncommon in Hungary, for in 1843 the country's Jews (though still kept within their ghettos) began to conduct all their secular affairs in Hungarian. They became Hungarian patriots, and were esteemed as such by nationalists such as

Kossuth and Deák. After 1848 many Jews took Hungarian names, others began to spell their Hebrew names in Hungarian style.

So it was not anti-semitism that sent Rudolph on his wanderings, but a desire to better himself. These wanderings, a veritable odyssey, were often recalled afterwards to his son: 'Szombathely, Vienna, Budapest, Milan, London, Dublin.' He reached London in 1865, but by the spring of the same year, he was already in Dublin.

There he met and married Ellen Higgins, about whom little can now be discovered, in the summer of 1865. Ellen Higgins was the daughter of one Julius Higgins, who had been born Karoly, also in Hungary and also of Jewish origins. He had married a girl of real Irish descent named Fanny Hegarty. Perhaps this strong middle European connection explains the otherwise curious attraction to an Irish girl of the newly arrived foreigner.

Somewhere in the background of these dark-skinned, dark-haired Virags and Karolys lurked the Teutonic blondness of Freiherr von Hauptmann Hainau, an officer in the Imperial Austrian Army. Hainau was imprisoned by the Emperor, according to family tradition. But what brought a well-connected officer to the dark cells of the Viennese despot was forgotten. His colour was to come out later, by one of those queer genetic sports, in Leopold Bloom's own child Milly, the blonde daughter of dark parents.

So various and complex are the strands of history and heredity that we should not be surprised to find a Wandering Jew having an Irish destination.

Rudolph Virag, now established in Dublin, was received into the Church of Ireland by the Society for Promoting Christianity among the Jews, before his marriage to Ellen Higgins in August 1865. The Rev. Thomas Wellard, the minister who instructed him, was kindness itself during their several talks at 12 Sackville Street.

Before this Rudolph inserted this notice in the press:

I, Rudolph Virag, now resident at No. 52 Clanbrassil Street, Dublin, formerly of Szombathely in the Kingdom of Hungary, hereby give notice that I have assumed and intend henceforth upon all occasions and at all times to be known by the name of Rudolph Bloom.

For the world in general, May 1866 was marked by the appearance in the night sky of a nova, a brilliant stellar apparition; privately for the Blooms by the birth of a son they named Leopold Paula Bloom. The boy was baptised into the reformed Protestant faith of the Church of Ireland by the Rev. Mr Gilmer Johnson, M.A., in the parish church of St Nicholas Without, in the Coombe. As the father's change of name became official at the same time, father and son became Dubliners at the same time.

The area of Dublin in which Rudolph Bloom had settled himself was not casually chosen. Already at that date it was by way of being the Jewish quarter of Dublin, though it was by no means a ghetto, as that term might describe the walled-in settlements of Judaism in Hungary and elsewhere.

The Dolphin's Barn area was then largely new and the streets had become a natural place for newcomers to find a home. The names of Central Europe hung over the shop fronts, foreign foods mixed with plain Irish fare, Yiddish accents were confused with the flat tones of the native Dubliners.

There had been an original Jewish community in Dublin, going back several centuries, but there was a distance, even a coolness between them and these 'newcomers'. Soon, however, many of the new arrivals from Germany, Russia and Hungary were established in small businesses — as was Rudolph Bloom himself — easily finding ways to support themselves, however humbly.

The Blooms' home, however, was an older Georgian house, on a road leading out of the city over the Grand Canal. It was large enough for a family of three and a servant. Among the early memories retained by Leopold Bloom — broken fragments of a lost past — were some of his father and of their home.

At six he recalled his father (then in his late fifties) relating the events of his wandering life. It seemed from what his father said that, for the Jew, wandering was an inevitable fate. The small boy would follow his father's narrative, poring over the railway lines of Europe worked out on his atlas map.

His father would give him advice: 'take care of the pence and the pounds will take care of themselves.' Trade was his

11

life. And, in turn, the boy suggested the establishment of a chain of shops in the towns of Europe through which his father had passed.

His first steps in improving his mind were taken at a dame's school run by Mrs Ellis — where he learnt to play marbles. Mrs Ellis, he remembered, had a taste for mignotte lace. The child was always of a speculative turn of mind: at eight he began to ponder, as he was to ponder all his life, that queer conundrum: 'Where was Moses when the candle went out?'

Going to bed at night he would review the day's events, sitting on his bed picking the scabs off his knees and the bits from between his toe jambs. A brief bend of the knee, a short prayer, and long ambitious meditations on the future before him. He was Leopold Bloom of Clanbrassil Street but also

> Ellpodbomool
> Molldopeloob
> Bollopedoom
> Old Ollebo MP

It would be fun to be an MP, a Member of Parliament. But the child also had his present tensions — he was a bed-wetter. His mother would put on the rubber sheet over the mattress, the rubber sheet with a queer smell.

Dear mother: she had lavished her love on him, but for Leopold in later years her memory was almost totally eclipsed by her husband, his father.

Leopold was a solitary child, given to solitary play. In the afternoons, home from school, he often sat in the front room observing through a rondel of bossed glass in the multi-coloured pane the spectacle offered by the world outside, the pedestrians, horses, cycles, vehicles, all drawn out of shape, passing round the red rim of the glass.

He had literary ambitions, though, at an early age. At eleven he entered a poetry competition run by the *Shamrock* with three prizes, none of which he carried away with the following effort:

> An ambition to squint
> At my verses in print
> Makes me hope that for these you'll find room.

12

If you so condescend
Then place at the end
The name of yours truly, L. Bloom.

The editor, the notorious Richard Pigott who later forged
letters to link Parnell with terrorism, didn't print the poem.

When he was thirteen or fourteen, Leopold paid in for
himself to see Albert Hengler's *Grand Cirque* in its annual
visit to the Rotunda. This was a delightful show, with the
Whimsical Walker and his donkey; Handy Andy who wrought
havoc by well-meant efforts to help his colleagues, and the
Water Novelty with the arena filled up with water and
played on by boats and gondalas. Sometimes there were
special events such as Turpin's Ride to York on Black Bess,
and, even more thrilling, the South Wales Borderers defending
Rorke's Drift against the Zulu hordes in 1879.

These scenes remained vivid in his memory, and not only
because of the thrills. The trapese artists often terrified
him lest they fall to their deaths by missing the bar and
plunging into the sawdust below. He would bury his head
in his hands.

Then the clowns came on. One of these, with parti-coloured
face and fancy costume, came up into the audience, looking
for someone. He came to where Bloom sat alone, and
announced to the whole crowd that he (Bloom) was his (the
clown's) father. Cheers and laughter rocked the crowd.
Leopold cringed.

'No, no,' he cried, unheard. 'I'm not his father.'

But in later years, brooding over the irreparability of
the past, it came back to him in memory as it never could
in life. Too late to mend. The clowns went on by some
mysterious reincarnation; some subtle metempsychosis
produced them as it produced trapese artists. But little
boys had real fathers, real fears to face, real deaths to find.

At the age of twelve, in 1878, he was promoted, educationally,
to the High School in Harcourt Street.

Founded in 1870 by the Trustees of Erasmus Smith, the
seventeenth-century planter, for the education of middle-
class Protestant boys, the school was hardly old enough
then to have traditions — which was perhaps as well. It was

13

housed in a bleak eighteenth-century brick house, with a small playground full of mud and pebbles, fenced along the street side by a high iron railing and granite wall. It faced the ornamental facade of Harcourt Street railway station, squalid with the scattered rubbish of Wicklow peasants in their frieze coats, and a long advertising hoarding, from which posters implored the boys to consider the benefits of Sunlight Soap, and the thrills of Poole's Myriorama.

Here Leopold absorbed the usual quota of subjects: Latin, English, Maths and Science. Like all his contemporaries he had to compose a weekly essay, one some topic such as 'My Favourite Hero', 'Procrastination is the Thief of Time', or 'Men may rise on the stepping-stones of their dead selves to higher things'. No one gave much heed to disciplined decorum and the boys worked in a din of voices. The school day began with prayers in the Clock Room. The headmaster, Mr Wilkins, would pass through the routine religious observances, but when class began, if he were in the mood, he would joke about the Church and the views of the Clergy. He took a modern view: 'let them say what they like, the earth does go round the sun.'

Leopold, in view of this general attitude, was deeply impressed by the science master, Mr Vance, who left the boy with a lifelong interest in scientific ideas. The mysteries of gravity, the law of falling bodies, the range of the spectrum in light. The mnemonic for this last — ROYGBIV — he remembered after many years: red, orange, yellow, green, blue, indigo, violet. Also acoustics, the properties of sound, the action of heat, magnetism.

There were no bullies at High School — another benefit of newness. The boys from families where money mattered, and who had their eyes on a future in the army, the civil service or India, worked hard. Indeed no one ever asked Leopold, 'Who is your father?', expecting him to be a gentleman or a magistrate. This was no snob school like Clongowes or Belvedere.

The staff reflected this as well. William Wilkins, the headmaster (only the second the school had ever had), had taken honours at Trinity and wrote poetry in his spare time. His brother George was a large bluff man who reminded the

14

boys of Holbein's Henry VIII. He was an easy-living sybarite, but later on took holy orders and became a Fellow of Trinity to the surprise of many he had taught.

There was nothing fancy about this practical-minded school. One old boy later complained that Shakespeare was read only for the grammar. But other subjects were treated with a little humour. Bloom carried away, as almost his only memory of the language, the following version of 'Humpty Dumpty' in Latin:

> *Humptaeus Dumptaeus summa tenens sedet,*
> *Humptaeus Dumptaeus pracipitans cadit;*
> *Equitum peditum milia milens*
> *Humptaeum Dumptaeum tollere non queunt.*

But all was not lessons. In the two-acre playground was a ball alley and gym apparatus — as well as a flagpole from which the Union Jack could be flown on feast days of the Empire. The playing fields for football and cricket, as well as the rifle range, were out in Belgrave Square. There, too, was the running track. Bloom at school was an athlete, though a poor one. The javelin was beyond him — he could not throw straight for his life. But he was good at gymnastics, especially on the parallel bars. Sports were important — even early in its history the school was outstanding at hurley.

The caretaker Kenny, in his straw hat, was the chief denizen of these areas. His long beard earned him the nickname 'Moses'. He was almost completely deaf and the subject of many jokes. Where was he, Bloom wondered, when the candles went out?

The masters too, made a mark. 'Tommy' the maths master, Mr T.W. Foote, who later became headmaster of the Royal Academy in Belfast. Tall, gaunt Mr W.S. Coony in his light-coloured trousers and fashionable Dundreary whiskers. The Rev. Oscar Kramer, Kramer the Crammer, the portly, long-haired modern languages master who died early.

But it is the boys who remain important for boys. Bloom's special friends were Percy Apjohn and Owen Goldberg. They called him Mackerel because of his green and blue stripped jersey: the three of them up the trees at Goose Green, playing at being monkeys. They were not the best examples of the evolution of intelligent life.

15

Years later Bloom would come across the names of other contemporaries who, according to the newspapers, were making their mark in the world. He always found it hard to believe that he had been at the same school as Harmsworth the journalist and Yeats the poet: they seemed queer enough products for any school. The law reports and business news featured other old boys, though the wars in India and South Africa took their toll, as in good time did the Great War. Others were merely wondered about: F. C. Day Lewis, who became a curate in Tuam: what did he ever achieve?

Slowly an awareness of the world beyond home and school grew up. A city of some 240,000 people did not then seem very crowded: one could walk from the city centre to the suburbs in twenty minutes or so. The idea of the city and its various people first came to Leopold on his way to school each morning.

With his satchel and his bread and cheese for lunch, he would kiss his mother goodbye and set off up Clanbrassil Street. On the corner was Leonard's emporium which sold everything one could imagine, groceries, ironwear, glass, coal and stamps from the Post Office. Here he came to the South Circular Road which led to Harrington Street, a street of red brick houses with newly painted doors and bright knockers — a respectable street. Past Longwood Avenue, Bloomfield Avenue, Synge Street; past the Catholic church. On Harrington Terrace he came to the Italian Warehouse, with all its continental delicacies — very different from the homely fare at Leonard's corner. Other shops in the neighbourhood sold those Jewish delicacies which his father still relished now and again.

Here he came to Kelly's corner, much busier with traffic in and out of town. In Harcourt Road was an institution which always caught his eye, the Shelter for Females Discharged from Prison. It seemed strange in the midst of all the houses, shops, and cabmen's stables.

Harcourt Street was mainly in the hands of professional men such as doctors and barristers with only an odd professor of music at the top end. Aside from the High School, there was also the Sacred Heart Convent, where the Rev. Mother Ashlin turned out her smart, respectable girls, all of

16

them the daughters of doctors and barristers (and a slight cut above the boys, many of whose fathers were in trade). The girls were separated from the boys by their religion — even more separated were the brethern who attended the Catholic Apostolic Church in Adelaide Road. They had very queer ideas, someone had told Leopold, but he found religion a perplexing thing. His father was only nominally a Protestant, and the boy could really be said not to have much conviction in the matter either. He would laugh at his father when as an old man he began reverting to Jewish customs. But his own lack of belief left Leopold something of an outsider, with both the boys and the girls.

As a youth Leopold had little luck with girls. He was, he thought, too ugly, a clumsy cod rather than a sleek mackerel. And yet: the fair-haired Lotty Clarke was observed with the aid of his father's opera glasses through ill-closed curtains going to bed. The same Lotty who rolled down the bank of the canal at Rialto Bridge tempting Leopold with her free flow of animal spirits, and a glimpse of her fleecy underwear. In the garden she climbed the crooked tree and the little demon possessed Leopold: he peeped between the flounces of her petticoat. Did it matter? No one knew.

And so, in due course, to other excesses of youth. The heat of growth in summer was relieved in a cattle creep behind Kilbarrack, under Ballybough Bridge and in the Devil's Glen. He was a precocious youth — shaved early — and saw this not as that foul and to be avoided sin of Onan, but as a sacrifice to the Fauns, the gods of the forest. In reality, when it was pairing time and impossible to mate, it satisfied a need.

All the boys were like him. One day Wilkins drew on the blackboard a portrait of Venus. It was something less than classical, leaving little to the imagination, her area of interest carefully delineated.

The year 1880 — marked in many minds by the burning down of the old Theatre Royal and the opening of St Stephen's Green as a public park — was Leopold's last year at school. For him that year was memorable for one remarkable feat: he was able to urinate higher than any of the 210 other pupils in High School, so winning an open competition at least once in his life.

17

He was, he found, sexually excitable. Very little sufficed to arouse him. A jaunting car, the mingling odours of the ladies' cloakroom and the gentlemen's lavatory, the thick throng mounting the stairs of the Royal, the theatre itself dark and sex-smelling. Even the price list in the paper of ladies' hosiery. He was a bad boy, but in the summer of 1880 there were sunspots, and they are well known to affect behaviour.

In Hatch Street, hurrying home from the theatre one night, he encountered his first prostitute. But the passing of two policemen on their round made the waif flee. Her name was Bridie Kelly, a country girl, and he dreamt of her.

The school play that year also provided an occasion not exactly of sin, but of sexual interest anyway. They were presenting a stage version of Anstey's popular novel *Vice Versa* about the misadventures of Mr Bultitude who magically changes places with his schoolboy son. Bloom was playing, in corsets supplied by his mother, the female role, the part of Dulcie, the headmaster's daughter. In the cast was his friend Gerald, and it was Gerald with the Stammer who converted him to a true corset lover. Gerald had the kink for girls' clothes from a fascination with his sisters' stays. (He was known as Ger-Ger from his impediment, and grew up to follow his bent by becoming an actor, all pinky greasepaint and gilded eyelids). Leopold too, fell for those mysterious garments and was never able to shrug off their allure.

On the annual school excursion that summer they went down to Poulaphouca. It was a hot heady day, and Bloom retired to the shade of the yews and masturbated. The luxury of it was sinful. Those were halcyon days. Percy Apjohn took his photograph later on: lying with his legs up, his hand resting on the bridge of his nose. A snapshot photograph of a lost day, recalling memories of lost friends: Donald Turnbull, Abraham Chatterton, Owen Goldberg, Jack Meredith, Percy Apjohn. Halcyon days.

And so out into the real world of work, into a city where modern change was under way. Already some streets were being prepared for electric lights which were switched on on 25 May 1881. They were almost enough to dissipate the fears

18

of childhood, and heighten the gay confidence of youth. In the 1880s a man could be anything he cared to be.

1880

Telford & Telford, Organ Builders to her Majesty, 109 St Stephen's Green, West. Established upwards of Forty Years. Every description of Church, Chancel, and Saloon Organ of very superior materials, finish and tone, at reasonable prices. Repairs and Tunings attended to in all parts of the country.

Wye House Asylum, Buxton, Derbyshire. An establishment for the care and treatment of the Insane of the Higher and Middle Classes. Resident Physician and Proprietor— F.K. Dickson, FRCP, Edin. Erected in 1861 by His Grace the Duke of Devonshire.

Tighe, Son, and Egan, Practical Patent Axle Manufacturers, 29 and 30, Temple-Bar, Dublin.

Thomas Dockrell, Sons, Martin, and Co. Execute in the Best Manner House Painting, Glazing, Paper Hanging, Gilding, Plumbing, Gasfitting, Hydraulic engineering, and marble works.

Stephen's Green Turkish, Electric & Medicated Baths, Dublin. In again drawing attention to the unique method of heating and ventilating adopted in these splendid baths, the proprietors wish to place the following important facts before the public:—
That no other Bath in Ireland is heated on this system by which Oxygenated Air is drawn from the heating chambers through the various rooms, and the whole of the Vitiated Air is carried off Downwards; thus ensuring a continuous

flow of Pure Heated Air, the great desideratum in a Turkish Bath. That, by this means, perfect circulation of air is established without the admission of Cold Air (which causes dangerous draughts) in to any of the hot rooms.

Turkish Baths, Russian Baths, Vapour Baths, Alkaline Baths, Sulphur Baths, Bran or Oatmeal Baths, Sanitas Baths, Salt-Water Baths, Iodine Baths, Nitro-Hydrochloric Baths,

and the Electric Baths

Alexander Thom & Co., Printers and Publishers. Irish National School Book Depot, 87, 88, & 89, Abbey Street, Dublin. Alexander Thom & Co. have always in stock the School Books published by the direction of the Commissioners of National Education in Ireland. They beg to call attention to the Commissioners' New Classification of their Illustrated Reading Books, which now embraces an Infants' Grade and Six Higher Classes.

2

Into the World

His friends planned careers in the army or civil service: young
Leopold's ambitions had been of a peculiar kind. His dream
was to become a shoefitter in Mansfield's shop in Grafton
Street. How sweet it would be, plying the button hook on
the long boots, laced up crossways to the knee, of the delicate
footed ladies of Clyde Road and Leeson Park. Passing daily
he admired the patent wax model Raymonde, her cobweb
hosiery and that long red toe, so daringly Parisian, he thought.

But the reality of work was different. He started life as a
salesman with his father, wearing his first hard hat. He was
the traveller for the family firm which sold fake jewellery,
equipped like all commercial travellers with his order book,
a scented handkerchief, a case of bright trinket samples and
a fund of funny stories.

He would ply his oily compliments on housewives young
and old, winning his commission before returning home.
His mother would be preparing the noodles for supper.
His father would be seated by the fire — the head of the
house as well as the firm — reading a paper from Central
Europe already a month old.

Soon, however, his father paid for an apprenticeship and
the young Bloom (now permanently promoted from Leopold) went to work in the mail-order room of David Kellet's
store in the new City Market buildings in South George's
Street. Bloom had to live in on the premises, along with the
rest of the unmarried staff, male and female. If nothing
else, young Bloom learnt there how to tie a knot.

His private interests did not wane. He spent the year
1882 studying the religious problem, and the summer months
trying to square the circle and thereby win a million pounds

(so he hoped). He was not the first, or last, deluded fool to follow that *ignis fatuus*. His ideas were permeated by the evolutionary theories of Charles Darwin, whose *Origin of Species* and *Descent of Man* were undermining the foundations of traditional faith. His ideas on evolution, religion and colonial expansion in Canada he expounded during long evening walks with his friends Francis Wade and David Magrane. But it was they who emigrated, Bloom who stayed.

1882 was memorable as the year of Bloom's only spree. At sixteen he joined a harriers club, with whom he got drunk one evening. Joining in a race, he fell, cut his head open and muddied himself up. He returned home to paternal anger and maternal sorrow. 'My poor son, he is going to rack and ruin. Drunk and filthy. Look at you. What will the neighbours say?'

But the neighbours in Clanbrassil Street had better things to talk about than the misadventures of young Bloom. For the country at large 1882 was marked by the horror of the Phoenix Park murders. The previous October Charles Parnell and others connected with the Land League had been arrested and detained in Kilmainham Jail. They were finally released on 2 May. On 6 May the new Lord Lieutenant arrived to be sworn in. The same afternoon the new Chief Secretary, Lord Frederick Cavendish, and the Under Secretary, Thomas Burke, were murdered while walking in the Phoenix Park.

The culprits were two members of a terrorist gang calling themselves the Irish National Invincibles. Approaching the two officials they stabbed them down, and while they lay wounded, cut their throats with surgical knives.

Those weapons gave the crime a peculiar *frisson*, but the whole affair was sensational. The murderers were driven to their appointment with death by a cab driver called Skin-the-Goat (so called because he was said to have sold the skin of a family pet while short of cash). The whole group were informed on by one of their own, James Carey, who turned queen's evidence. The murderers, Tim Kelly and Joe Brady, were duly hanged in Kilmainham. According to Dublin legend, Brady in death had to be cut down from the gallows with his penis standing up like a poker.

24

The whole country was in a political ferment over the agitations of the Land League and Parnell's parliamentary activities. Bloom, like most young men of his age, determined on setting the world to rights, was greatly excited by it all. In long evening walks in the couple of years that followed (while he was still at Clanbrassil Street), he talked all these things over with his friends Owen Goldberg and Cecil Turnbull between Longwood Avenue and Leonard's corner, Leonard's corner and Synge Street and Bloomfield Avenue. Round and round in the gathering twilight, they discussed music, literature, friendship, women, prohibition and a countless multitude of topics.

Other rambles were with Percy Apjohn, his friend from High School. Apjohn, whose people were from Limerick, lived out in Harold's Cross. Their walks nearly always ended at a wall between Gibraltar Villa and Bloomfield House, in Crumlin, just across the Grand Canal from Clanbrassil Street. To Apjohn, a scion of the landed gentry, Bloom expressed his support for the economic programme advocated by James Fintan Lalor, John Murray Fisher, John Mitchel, J.F.K. O'Brien and others, the agrarian policy of Michael Davitt, the constitutional agitation of Charles Stewart Parnell and the policies of William Ewart Gladstone. Bloom had become a staunch Home Ruler. The facts of Ireland's case were at his fingertips.

He wrote a prophecy of the consequences of Gladstone's Home Rule Bill in 1886 after an argument with Apjohn. This was sealed up in an envelope but never opened, as the measure failed to pass through the British parliament. Gladstone resigned, an event which caused much excitement in the city. The Tories were returned: Home Rule was lost. In Dublin, the bitterness of defeat was offset a little by the opening of the new Leinster Hall in Hawkins Street, on the site of the old Theatre Royal. This was yet another enterprise of Mr Michael Gunn.

By now Bloom had left Kellet's. In 1885 he obtained a position with the printers Alexander Thom and Sons, where he worked on the compiling of the *Post Office Directory for 1886*. This work was published every January based on information gathered the previous year. Much of it could be carried over, but painstaking work was required to get all the minute details correct.

In the year Bloom worked on this chore, there was some confusion over the valuation of the parochial houses of Star of the Sea church in Sandymount, numbers 3 and 5 Leahy's Terrace. Instead of being recorded as £28 valuation, they were inadvertently raised to £38, the valuation of the other houses in the row. But this error, which was not Bloom's fault — was detected and did not pass into print in the final directory, though many other peculiar errors did. In the pages of *Thom's* the dead arose and walked, men changed into women, women into men, and businesses long defunct flourished as in their heyday.

Thom's did many other kinds of work at their premises in Abbey Street. They printed the *Dublin Gazette*, the official government journal, as well as publications for public departments and also ordinary jobbing work. The works were pervaded by the smell of hot metal and warm glue.

But the free flights of youth were affected by the ties of family. His father's business had expanded from trinkets and baubles such as artificial diamonds to lending money and other dubious schemes. In Dublin as elsewhere, the immigrant Jew found himself tainted by money.

Having converted to the reformed faith of the Church of Ireland, Rudolph Bloom eventually returned to his ancestral religion, even reading over the *Haggada* to his son. He observed the ancient rites and rituals of the Jewish faith, though his emancipated son (fed on the novelties of the nineteenth century) scoffed at them.

Rudolph had, however, enough funds to acquire the Queen's Hotel in Ennis, Co. Clare. Clearly money-lending had proved more profitable than trinkets. But by now the old man was almost senile. He slept with his dog, and suffered from sciatica. To protect himself in winter he wore the skin of a tabby cat lining his heavy waistcoat. The dog, Athos, was as infirm as his master. Rudolph resorted to increasing doses of aconite to ease his neuralgia. His habits grew coarse. He ate without removing his hat, and sucked off his gooseberry fool from the plate, and would wipe his mouth with old envelopes or other scraps of paper.

He was given to belching after his dinner and to counting over his change shortsightedly. Money was, in fact, scarce, for the hotel in Ennis ruined him financially.

On 21 June 1886 Rudolph Bloom received the news of his wife's death in a Dublin nursing home. He was too ill to go up to Dublin and so she was buried by her son in a plot in Glasnevin. All that remained of his mother now was a brooch and her son's habit of carrying a potato to ward off disaster.

A week later a disaster came. On the evening of 27 June 1886, Rudolph Bloom retired to bed. He had bought a bottle of his neuralgic liniment that morning from Francis Dennehy, the chemist in Church Street. He also bought himself a new straw boater, which suggested he was in good form. However, that night he overdosed himself with the monkshood, leaving a note in an envelope marked *To My Dear Son Leopold*, in a sloping upright backhand.

> Tomorrow will be a week that I received the sad news of your mother's death. It is no use Leopold to be without one whom one has loved. I wish to be with your dear mother. Life is too long, that is not more to stand. I go to her, all for me is out of this life. Be kind to Athos, Leopold. My dear son, think always of me. Das Herz . . . Gott . . . dein . . .

They telegraphed for Leopold and he hurried down by train. He could not, however, bring himself to go into the room to look on the dead face of his father. Perhaps it was best for him, for them all.

There had, of course, to be an inquest. It was held on the afternoon of 28 June. On a table in the hotel room where the coroner sat, the red labelled aconite bottle stood in solitary menace. The room was hung with hunting pictures, and was stuffy and airless. The summer sun slanted through the wooden slates of the drawn Venetian blinds. Leopold, even in his distress, noted that the ears of the coroner (John Cullinan, Esq.) were huge, with wisps of hair emerging from their insides.

The boots from the Queen's gave evidence of finding the body. He had called Mr Bloom as usual, and thought he was asleep. Then he saw, like, yellow streaks down his face. The body had slipped down to the foot of the bed. It was unbearable.

The verdict was simple. Death by misadventure, due to the accidental ingestion of an overdose of aconite, self-administered. Sympathies were expressed to the son, and the letter addressed to him passed over. Mr Bloom was buried in Ennis, a lonely ceremony attended only by his son and a few people from the hotel.

For Bloom the death of his parents marked the end of an era — his meeting with his future wife the beginning of a new one.

1886

Support Home Trade. Collins and Graham, Wholesale Trunk and Joinery Works, Steam Saw Mills, Hanover Lane (Francis Street), Dublin. Commercial Travellers Sample Cases made to order and Repaired.

Dublin Whiskey Distillery Co., Limited. Jones' Road Distillery, Dublin. The most perfect "Pot Still" Distillery in the United Kingdom. No Patent Still on the Premises. No Foreign Barley Used, and none but the Finest Quality of Dublin Whiskey Made.

Dublin Society for the Prevention of Cruelty to Animals. The Object of this Society is to prevent cruelty and improper treatment of animals, and the Committee earnestly solicits the public generally, to transmit information of any gross case of Cruelty to Animals coming under their notice, to the Secretary, when prompt assistance will be cheerfully afforded, and every exertion made to facilitate the prosecution and punishment of the Offender.

The largest, cheapest, and most varied stock in the Kingdom at Farrell & Son, Glasnevin Marble Works. Headstones from 35s. Catalogues free.

Waller's Funeral and Carriage Establishment, 49 & 50, Denzille-street, Dublin.

Established 1830. Patrick Shalvey, General Horse Hair Manufacturer, Feather, Flock and Fibre Merchant and Purifier. 3 High Street, Dublin.

*House of St John of God, Stillorgan Castle, Dublin for the
Treatment of Mentally affected Gentlemen under the
Management of the Brothers of St John of God. The two
Medical Inspectors of Lunatic Asylums in Ireland have certi-
fied it to be the most perfect Institution of the kind they
know of, and one in which the patients have more personal
means of comfort, cheerful situation, and extensive pros-
pects, marine and inland.*

*Corry & Co.'s list comprises Soda, Potash or Kali, Lithia,
Carrara, and Cromac Seltzer Waters, Lemonade, Ginger
Ale, Aromatic Tonic, Sarsaparilla, Quinine, Summer and
Winter Beverages, Fruit Nectar, Hot Bitters, Etc., which
are admitted to be the most delicious Non-Alcoholic Bever-
ages extant.*

*Thousands are now living to testify to the Beneficent Effects
of* Dr Locock's Pulmonic Wafers, *which taste pleasantly.
15,293 cures of asthma, consumption, coughs, colds, bronchitis, and all disorders of the breath, throat and lungs,
rheumatism and heart complaints, have been published
in the last 12 months.*

*Isaac S. Varian & Co. Brush Manufacturers, North Dublin
Brush Factory, 91 & 92 Talbot Street.*

*Mons. Francois, Hairdresser, Perfumer, and Practical Wig
and Scalp Maker, 2 Nassau Street, 2. Best and leading house
in Dublin for all ornamental hair.*

*Brannick Brothers, manufacturers of charcoal, iron liquor,
etc. Kincora, Richmond Road, Drumcondra, Dublin.*

*John Kickney, Dealer in Horses and Job-Master, Lad Lane,
Lower Baggot-street. All orders receive strict attention.*

*Sculptors. First Prize Medal awarded Dublin Exhibition,
1882, to Pearse and Sharp, Ecclesiastical and Architectural
Sculptors, 27 Great Brunswick Street, and 155 & 156 Townsend Street, Dublin. Altars, Pulpits, Fonts, Statues, Carvings,
etc. Monuments, Tablets and all Kinds of Marble Work.*

3

Molly and Marriage

One evening in May 1887, at an entertainment at the home of Matt Dillon, on the Kimmage Road, Leopold Bloom met Miss Marion Tweedy.

Molly, as she was called by everyone there, was dressed in a yellow gown, with a black lace fichu. She was, he thought, the loveliest creature he had ever seen, certainly the prettiest one there that night. They played party games, he recalled, of the decorously boisterous kind, such as musical chairs. He followed around behind her. They were the last couple out, but she reached the chair before him, bubbling with laughter.

And then: then they sang. Standing at her shoulder he turned the music while she played and sang *Waiting*, the scent of her lilac toilet water filling his senses, her bosom heaving as she sang:

> The stars shine on his pathway, the trees bend back
>   their leaves,
> To guide them to the meadow among the golden
>   sheaves,
> Where stand I, longing, loving and listening as I wait,
> To the nightingale's wild singing, singing, sweet singing
>   to its mate.

Bloom turned the sheet to the last page, eyeing Molly's full bosom.

> I hear his foot-falls music,
> I feel his presence near,
> All my soul, responsive, answers
> And tells me he is here;

O stars, shine out your brightness,
O nightingales, sing sweet.
To guide him to me, waiting
And speed his flying feet.

She thanked him for his courtesy, and Leopold was caught up in his fate by those deep Spanish eyes.

May 1887 was in retrospect a momentous date in the life of Leopold Bloom. After that first meeting, Leopold and Molly often met at Matt Dillon's house. Dillon was an open-hearted, hospitable man. One evening a garden party was arranged, with a game of bowls. Bloom, more by chance than by skill, triumphed over a young lawyer named John Henry Menton.

The air was scented with lilac blossom which hung heavy from the grove at the end of the garden, where Molly stood arm in arm with Dillon's bevy of girls, Floey, Tiny, Atty, Sara, Nannie and Mamie. They were holding up on the urn a lad of four or five in a Lord Fauntleroy suit, who frowned at the fear of falling. The lad glanced back to his mother, who sat with the Dillons on the veranda outside the house.

Matt Dillon congratulated Bloom: 'An easy win, Poldy. Come up here and meet Mrs Dedalus and her husband Simon. Oh yes, and this is their eldest, Stephen. Say hello Stephen to the conquering hero.'

But the boy frowned again, and hid his hand, refusing to shake hands with the stranger.

'Ah and here are the girls! Come in now. There is a cold chicken laid out, with some nice cigars and some special brandy for you men after your exertions. Bad luck, John. You were beaten well and truly there by Bloom.'

Molly and her special friend Floey passed into the house, followed by Bloom and Menton and the rest of the party. In the candlelight the solid silver service on the sideboard reflected the good spirits of Matt Dillon.

Floey later married an architect; Atty was jilted by a lawyer in the Four Courts; and Mamie, the religious one, went out to Spain.

Menton lost more than a game of bowls to Bloom: he lost over Molly as well; not that Molly minded, for much later, after Menton had married, she saw him flirting with some girl at Poole's Myriorama. Menton would not have been a good match for her, though he recalled her fondly years later to a friend. ('A fine looking woman, and a good armful with plenty of game in her. What did she want to marry a coon like that for?')

Soon after Bloom called on the Tweedys at the house in Rehoboth Terrace, not a difficult address to find as the house was only one of three (one of which was the Post Office for Dolphin's Barn). Her father was a retired army man. He called himself Major Tweedy, though some in Dublin, such as Simon Dedalus, called him a drum major. He had been in the Royal Dublin Fusiliers. He was a pipe smoker and a heavy drinker, and talked endlessly of military campaigns, such as the Battle of Plevna, in such a way that you would have thought he had been there. Bloom, whose knowledge of many events in Central Europe beyond the Danube was hazy, never got the old man's career straight in his head.

Indeed, Bloom had only the haziest ideas about Molly's background. She had been born in Gibraltar in 1870, some seventeen years before, in the month of September. Her father had been out there with the army. Her mother, it seems, was Spanish. Her name was Lunita Laredo, but she died when Molly was an infant. From her Molly inherited her eyes and her figure. She had begun singing in Gibraltar, but the year before they had to return to Dublin on the Major's retirement. For a child reared in the hot exotic ambience of the Mediterranean, Dublin seemed cold, damp and depressing.

All that long summer and into the winter Leopold wooed Molly. There were more parties at the Dillons, and at the home of Luke and Catherine Doyle at Camac Place. In June 1887 he kissed Molly for the first time after charades at Luke Doyle's. Down among the night-scented stock at the dark end of the garden, he bent to kiss her lips and her shoulder above her heart.

The Dillons and Doyles were impressed with Bloom. He spoke volubly of his ideals, of setting the country on its feet, of standing for parliament in the Home Rule interest. The young Bloom had very grand ideals indeed, even to asking Molly to learn and sing a French song from *Les*

Hugenots, because he lamented the religious persecution they had suffered. Terrible things, he said, were done for the sake of religion.

The song extolled the beauties of Touraine, but had to be heard alongside such performances as those by Simon Dedalus, in which the verses got mixed up and the tune went astray. At one charade Bloom did Rip van Winkle: a ripped coat, a bread van, cockles and periwinkles. Twenty years asleep, returning to find all changed, the young grown old. But that summer, at sixteen, Molly had little thought of old age, as she leant against the sideboard watching him, delighted by his sense of fun.

And after that first kiss in the garden, he had sat upon the wall to watch the sunrise, noting all the changes that heralded the first light of dawn and a new day. And a new era for Bloom!

Part of that new day was Molly's growing affection for what he had long thought of as his ugly person. Her love gave him a personal confidence he had long lacked. When she said how she admired Byron, Bloom would have to give himself Byronic airs. Kind and polite though her Poldy may have been, he was no heroic poet.

In January, on old Christmas Night, they were guests at the housewarming of Georgina Simpson and her husband. Also there was Josie Powell, the prettiest deb in Dublin despite her buckteeth. She was Molly's best friend, but she also harboured feelings for Leopold. After the games of finding the pin and thought reading, there was dancing. Josie was sitting out as a wallflower. Bloom took pity on her and asked her to dance, and then sat out with her on the staircase ottoman. Molly was furious when she came on the scene. But it was only later, when Bloom was going on about Jesus being the first socialist, that they had a row, a real stand-up row.

'Don't be silly Poldy, that's just nonsense.'

'No, Molly dear. I'm serious. What does He say about the rich, and sharing and loving your neighbour. . .'

'And holding hands with Josie Powell, I suppose that's socialism too, is it?'

'What do you mean? Poor thing, left a wallflower.'

'Wall weed more likely, if I know that one.'

34

'Now, now, Molly don't be silly. You know I care only for you. You know that.'

It was soon made up, but Molly pretended to Bloom that she had fallen out with Josie over him. She knew, of course, that he was wild about her. And he *had* looked handsome that night, in his dinner jacket, with water-silk facings, black bow-tie and mother-of-pearl cuff links, a blue masonic pin in his buttonhole (quite contrary to the rules of the order). He had proposed the toast, with raised champagne glass in hand, so charmingly:

'Ladies and gentlemen, I give you Ireland, home and beauty.'

In February Bloom's thoughts turned to Valentine's Day. He sent Marion a card with an acrostic verse:

> Poets oft have sung in rhyme
> Of music sweet their praise divine.
> Let them hymn it nine times nine.
> Dearer far than song or wine,
> You are mine. The world is mine.

And to Josie Powell he sent one too, of a fleet gazelle.

The relationship between Molly and Poldy became more intimate. She lent him a book out of which tumbled the photo of a young man in uniform: a mystery man about whom Bloom could not bring himself to ask. He presented her with a volume of Byron's poems and three pairs of gloves. He was interested in her life in quite intimate ways. He kissed her in the eye of her glove and made her take it off.

'Is it permitted to ask the shape of your bedroom?' he asked one evening in Kenilworth Square. And then, 'I beg you, let me have a little snip off the edge of your drawers.' He slipped the glove into his pocket while she coped with these queries. Eventually she gave him a pair of drawers off her doll. Bloom was mad about drawers.

The Tweedys had by now left Rehoboth Terrace to take a house in Brighton Square. One day when ink got on his hands he requested permission to wash them in the basin in her bedroom, which looked out over the rere garden to the back lane. He used the Albion Milk and sulphur, but the whole thing was just a pretext to see where she slept.

And yet he felt things were getting too warm. He stayed

away from the house for a while. But then she met him in Harold's Cross Road, looking very smart in a Zingari scarf, which set off his colouring. He said her openwork sleeves must be cold in such weather. He begged her to raise the hem of her skirt so he could glimpse the orange petticoat she was wearing. Mad, she thought, quite mad.

One night in the kitchen of Brighton Square he almost proposed. But she was pretending to be in a temper with the flour on her hands from the potato cakes she was making. The moment passed. Though he wrote constantly, he took a little prodding to the point. Molly and Josie were always teasing him, hugging and kissing while he was there, just to arouse him.

Then in May 1888 (a year after they had met), on an excursion to Howth Head, Bloom finally proposed. They took the train out to Sutton Station and then the tram up to the summit. Lying in the wild ferns looking out over the blue distant sea, he asked and she said, after a moment, yes she would. He kissed her then, and she, with rising passion, kissed him back.

Accepted now by Molly, to marry her he must be received into the Catholic Church. The Jewish Hungarian Irish Protestant Masonic freethinker would have to be converted. The parish priest was approached and a course of instruction followed so that early in October Leopold Bloom could be baptised a Catholic by the Rev. Charles Malone, C.C., at the Church of the Three Patrons in Rathgar.

The couple planned to marry on the 8 October. A month before Bloom sent Molly eight poppies for her birthday. She had by now told him something of her mother's history, which was not really as respectable as could have been desired, he gathered, but he did not care. She had other worries though: a white vaginal discharge was disturbing her. She went to Dr Collins on Pembroke Road, a specialist in women's diseases, on Floey Dillon's prompting. His medical enquiries, couched in suitable jargon, gave her a clean bill of health at the cost of a guinea.

By now their relationship was more intimate, passing early beyond mere kissing. Two days after, Molly came round to see the shape of his bedroom and they made love, while at home the Major waited for his dinner. Much to

Molly's disappointment, Poldy was not circumcised. A few weeks after, failing her period, Molly realised she must be pregnant. She told Leopold, who worried away at this new problem.

On 8 October 1888, they married in the same church, the Three Patrons in Rathgar.

They received the usual assortment of wedding presents. Alderman John Hooper, a political associate of Leopold's, presented them with a stuffed owl. The Dillons, with a more friendly attention to practicality and the difficulty of dusting, gave them a clock set in green Connemara marble. From the Doyles came a dwarf tree, a hardy Alpine growth, queerly suited to their way of life. As Molly said at the time, with a stuffed owl what more could they want?

Marriage changes many things: old ways are altered, old friends changed for new. For Bloom there was a new job, in Mr Wisdom Hely's emporium in Dame Street; for Molly, a sloughing off of Josie Powell; for both a new home, in Pleasants Street, off Camden Street.

Hely's were wholesale and manufacturing stationers with large premises in Dame Street, a shop long familiar to Dubliners, for in later years, they branched out into other fields such as toys and sporting guns. Bloom's employer, Charles Wisdom Hely, had inherited the business from his father, Charles Barden Hely. He lived out in a large, comfortable house, Linwood, in Sydney Parade. Mr Hely was a prominent gentleman in the city, rising by 1904 to be a justice of the peace, with a house on Highfield Road and another on Coliemore Road in Dalkey. Bloom was employed as a traveller in the stationary lines made by the firm — 'a traveller in blotting paper' as John Henry Menton later described him (still smarting from the loss of Molly). The job gave Bloom a certain level of security to set up home on his own.

Though Molly drifted out of her friendship with Josie Powell (largely because Josie herself soon married Denis Breen), in their neighbourhood she and Poldy had a friendly circle of acquaintances, mainly among the Jewish community that was so strong around there.

Among these friends were the Citrons, Ethan Mastiansky

and Nisan Moisel. Israel Citron (who only died in 1951) was a trader on the weekly payments system, selling drapery and clothes, who lived at 17 St Kevin's Parade. Ethan Mastiansky lived in 2 Mater Street, and he too was in the drapery trade. Nisan Moisel of Arbutus Place — he provided Bloom with the information about the retail quality and price of citrons — worked as a grocer and poultry dealer. His son, Elyah Wolf Moisel, was married to Basseh Hodess — who gave birth to a daughter on 28 June 1889. Bloom often recalled Molly and Mrs Moisel with bellies out, pregnant — for Milly Bloom was born the same month. Wolf Moisel died in 1904 of pyemia — one of a number of friends who died about that time.

And there were other friends: Goldwater, Rosenberg, Watchman, Abramovitz, Chazen — a roll-call of the Jewish race. With these Bloom could discuss his favourite topics — and himself impart casual information, such as that the best opium poppies grew in Chinese cemeteries.

Molly too gained curious information: from Mrs Mastiansky she learnt of her husband's preference for rere entry in copulation. It was in Pleasants Street that her own husband attempted this 'ultimate obscenity', and, under Irish law, criminal offence.

Molly had married pregnant. The child of that hasty copulation was born on 15 June 1889. As Molly's pains came on, Bloom had to hurry out into the night for Mrs Thornton, the midwife, and for Dr Murren, the physician, whom Molly had been attending. The lively child was named Milly.

After the birth Molly recovered quickly. She had an abundance of milk, and Bloom even considered putting her out to hire as a wet nurse at a pound a week. But Molly would not be treated like a milch cow. Her figure, now fuller, was duly admired by a student lodger of the Citron's named Penrose, who passed the house at convenient moments. After weaning the baby, she still suffered some discomfort because she had so much milk, and had to have a belledonna prescription to ease the pain. She put on nine pounds after Milly was born, a rise in weight which was only a fraction of her future gain.

Soon there was a return to a gay social life, which included an outing to the newly opened racecourse at Leopardstown. With them went Josie Powell. Molly, with a run of luck, won seven shillings. Others in the party included Mick Rogers and the Maggot O'Reilly — so called because he was always acting the fool. Mrs Joe Gallaher was kind enough to share her spiced beef sandwiches with Molly. Bloom found he was still attracted by the handsome and fashionably dressed Josie: a disturbing experience for a married man with a new baby. But these excitements of their private life, these harmless avocations of their time and class, were soon eclipsed by the greater excitements of public life.

In November 1890 the divorce suit of Captain William O'Shea against his wife was heard; the leader of the Irish Parliamentary Party, Charles Stewart Parnell, was named as co-respondent.

The evidence in the case was followed with relish by newspaper readers all over the world. The political events in Ireland had come to bore most people. But sordid sexual intrigue was easily relished by all. Only rarely did a scandal of such proportions explode upon the staid public life of Victorian Britain. The Cleveland Street Affair the year before had been sordid enough — indeed impinged so closely on the royal family with its horrid buggery of messenger boys by bluebloods, that it were better hushed up. But no one was going to hush up the sexual pecadilloes of an Irish leader as revealed in open court.

The Blooms and their friends followed the case and argued its merits. All were agreed that Captain O'Shea was a scoundrel, in the same class as that rogue Pigott. But the love of Parnell and Katharine O'Shea was not really so sensational as the romantics would have wanted. When it was not a little cheap with its assignations, it was trite, with its little place in Brighton and three children. For Leopold Bloom it was all tremendous: showing at least one Irish politician to be a man of parts.

When the decree *nisi* was granted on 17 November 1890, the real trouble began. Parnell was prepared to fight. Mr Bloom read in the *Freeman's Journal* on 18 November 'that Mr Parnell has not the remotest intention of abandoning either permanently or temporarily, his position or his duties as leader of the Irish Parliamentary Party.' He read it out to Molly at breakfast, while she sipped her tea in bed.

'You'll see,' he said, 'the people will stick by him.'

'That's all very well. But what will the priests say? You men are all romantics. You'll see: the priests will have the last word.'

It then emerged that Gladstone's Liberal Party, Parnell's parliamentary allies, threatened to break with the Irish Party unless a new leader was found. The Irish were presented with a stark choice between Parnell and Home Rule, for without Liberal support they had no parliamentary leverage. At an impassioned meeting in Committee Room 15 of the House of Commons, the party voted to replace Parnell. His defiant message to the Irish people was, 'I will fight to the end.'

Dublin was excited by Parnell's appearance there, but for Mr Bloom, 11 December 1890 was more than exciting. Parnell's first act was to see that the party newspaper, *United Ireland*, which had gone against him, was taken over. But while Parnell was addressing a rally at the Rotunda, his enemies recaptured the newspaper building. The next morning Parnell (before departing for Cork), attended by a huge crowd, swept down on the newspaper office to recover it.

Bloom that morning had got up early to go about his business. He was passing down O'Connell Street when he got caught by the crowd converging on Lower Abbey Street. He was carried with them, sensing that from the cries of 'Up Parnell' something momentous was now afoot. Outside the offices of *United Ireland*, now barred and bolted, there were wild scenes, sticks and revolvers being brandished to add menace to the verbal threats hurled at the miscreants inside.

Then around the corner càme a pony carriage with two men in it, the well-known Dr Kenny, and with him, Parnell himself. Bloom had seen Parnell once before in the flesh, addressing a meeting in Ennis, and had been overcome by his powerful, electric personality. Cheers filled the air, added to the threats and abuse of the Chief's enemies. The carriage pulled up so quickly that the horse was thrown down. Parnell leapt down and ran up the steps. He banged on the door, demanding admittance. But the door stayed closed, taunts and jeers coming from those within.

Pale with passion, his dark eyes flaming, Parnell resolved to storm the building. Bloom heard him send his men for a crowbar and pickaxe. These were soon brought. A discussion followed. Then Parnell exclaimed that if the hall doors were bolted, the area door might be forced. He would have jumped down and tried it himself, but he was restrained.

'Go yourselves' he cried, 'if you will not let me.'

Several of his men dropped down and forced the door. Parnell then snatched up the crowbar and attempted the main door. It gave way under his forceful batterings, and followed by those nearest to him, he swept into the house. Bloom was carried along with them.

Pandemonium broke out. Fierce cries and shouts, the trampling of feet up the uncarpeted stairs. The enemies of the Chief put up only a token resistance in the end, but he was thrown about, his well-brushed coat getting covered in dust, his hat flying off in the fray.

Bloom, retreating from the violence of this fracas, retrieved the fallen hat and dusted it off on the sleeve of his coat. Upstairs a window was removed and Parnell appeared. He had won. A great cheer greeted him. His face was deathly pale with vivid red spots on his cheeks, a vivid unhealthy colour. He looked fearsome and when he spoke his voice was terrible.

'I rely on Dublin. Dublin is true. What Dublin says today, Ireland will say tomorrow.'

As Parnell came out of the house, Bloom went up to him.

'Your hat, Mr Parnell.'

'Thank you' said Parnell, turning on him those fearful dark eyes, still alive with the storm of his passion. Bloom was electrified. The moment passed — Parnell mounted his carriage, and followed by the raucous crowd, set off down the quays to Kingsbridge to catch the train to Cork.

Bloom, too excited now to think of work, followed. At the station the crowd ignored the protests of the inspectors and poured onto the platform. Parnell got into a saloon carriage, and standing at the window waved to the crowd. By now he was pale, tired, exhausted. Beside him Bloom heard a girl cry out to her father, 'Oh, father, hasn't he a lovely face?'

Then Parnell was gone. The train whistled and to the renewed cheers of the crowd pulled out of the station. Less than a year later he was dead.

All through the following year, 1891, Parnell had fought to regain his position as the undisputed leader of the Irish Party. But the force of Liberal opinion in England (fearful of a general election in which they might be allied to such a notorious immoralist) and clerical authority in Ireland was against him. While still heavily engaged with his enemies, he died suddenly at Brighton on 6 October 1891.

He had failed to take precautions to change his wet clothing after a meeting, and had contracted pneumonia on top of a weak heart and rheumatic fever. He was only forty-five when he died. The public funeral in Dublin was made an occasion of great solemnity. A phase of Irish history had ended.

Reading the account of the funeral in his *Freeman's Journal* Bloom wondered at it all. The passion, the intrigue, the fanaticism, the sudden death: it was like some play written for the Gaiety rather than real life. He looked up at Molly brushing her hair in the chair by the window. All for love was it? Was passion then the paramount affection of the heart? Or had Parnell allowed his weakened moral feeling to betray that greater affection, love of country?

'A sad business,' he said.

'It's her I feel sorry for,' said Molly. 'Parnell gone, left a widow with three children,'

As was Ireland, thought Bloom and many others that Christmas. It might well be a long time before another man like Parnell appeared. Indeed Bloom heard it rumoured that Parnell was not dead, that they had buried a coffin full of rocks. Parnell, it was said, was alive. Parnell would come again.

To many of his acquaintances at this time Bloom's own politics were largely a mystery. As most of them regarded the political system as a means to an end, namely their own careers, his queer eccentric views were regarded askance. You couldn't take the man seriously, Alderman Hooper used to say. Bloom had worked hard in ward politics to get Hooper elected, a difficult enough task in Dublin. But Bloom thought he deserved more. He would run himself for alderman; he would become lord mayor; he would stand for parliament in the Home Rule interest. And, said Simon Dedalus, if Bloom had his way, he would be crowned High King of Ireland on Tara Hill.

But Bloom's politics were largely a matter not so much of fantasy as wishful thinking. If he had considered it seriously he would have realised that few votes in Dublin would go to a Jewish Irish Protestant converted to Catholicism who was reported to be an agnostic Freemason. Protestantism he would get away with. Jewish race, just about. But Freemasonry and Agnosticism would never do. Yet in his own idealistic way, Bloom felt himself that he would have had a great deal to offer Dublin as lord mayor, and the country itself as an MP. He at least, he reflected, after the fall of Parnell, he at least was honest. But after Parnell's death, the heart went out of politics for many people like Bloom. The Irish in Westminster were divided, at home the factions squabbled away among themselves. Practical minded men — men like William Martin Murphy — gave themselves over to commercial enterprises and agricultural improvement. This was real, this was progress. Politics had become a ridiculous and sordid game. Looking back, Bloom could see he was well out of it. He had his small platoon in Molly and Milly — that was enough responsibility for one man.

But when he saw Val Dillon or Tim Harrington dressed up in their finery going about their official duties or receiving guests at the Mansion House, he felt a small twinge of regret. It would have been a fine thing for the son of an immigrant to have risen to be lord mayor of Dublin — the first Jewish mayor in the city's history. It would have been a fine thing — but he knew such a thing would not be seen in his lifetime.

By 1892 the Blooms were resident at 38 Lombard Street West, where they lived for nearly two years. This street gave out on to Lower Clanbrassil Street, and was only a step away from their old house. The street was not quite as attractive, but was, at least, busier. These were happy years, made happier for Molly by the discovery of a new experience — the achievement of a complete climax. Previously, so she imagined, Bloom must have put himself into the wrong

43

place. She was now twenty-two and a complete woman.

She still kept up her singing, by joining the choir in the local church. There she became acquainted with the well-known tenor Bartell D'Arcy. One evening after practice, he offered to walk her home. She waited for him while he settled a point about the arrangement with the organist. She had been singing Gounod's *Ave Maria*. While they came down the choir stairs, the organ swelling above them, D'Arcy kissed her. For all his weedy voice, he could use his mouth with passion. She never told Bloom about this. He considered Bartell D'Arcy, who wore waxed moustaches, a conceited fellow, too fond of his own talent.

In January 1892 Bloom himself encountered, for the second time, young Stephen Dedalus in the coffee room of Breslin's Hotel, with his father and granduncle. Stephen was now almost ten years old, and asked Mr Bloom with gravity whether he would like to dine with them. Bloom gracefully declined.

Milly was growing. Bloom thought her a delightful creature; even her small sensitive hands moved him deeply. She too was a person of feeling. She buried a small dead bird in the kitchen matchbox, putting a daisy chain and bits of broken china on the grave. He called her Silly Milly; she called herself Padney Socks.

They seemed, in those days, to have more friends, like the Comerfords who invited them to their party in the cold winter of 1893 (always remembered by Molly because she had to make use of a men's toilet on the way home, having eaten too many oranges and drunk too much lemonade). She had her concerts, too, one, she remembered, on a cold night when Professor Goodwin made a botch of his piano music.

Every few months Professor Goodwin would present a farewell concert. Molly sang at many of these, accompanied by the slightly drunk, wholly aged musician. Once he called to Lombard Street of an afternoon while she was hot and flushed from standing over a steaming stew, and she had felt very bedraggled. The professor was most respectful and took no heed of her fluster — they had no maid then to answer the door.

One of these concerts was memorable for the complete

lack of proper arrangements, a hold up Molly called it. Held in the oak room of the Mansion House, it attracted a large audience. Coming away that night Goodwin was walking ahead of Bloom with Molly on his arm up Harcourt Street. Her sheet music blew out of Bloom's arms and was flattened by the wind against the High School railings. Loose sheets slipped through and were gusted away into the darkness. Dimly he could see the school buildings, once so familiar and warm with gas on winter days, now darkened and strange.

He hurried after the couple, and as they turned the corner of Harcourt Street, the wind blew up Molly's skirt, and whipped her long boa off her shoulder and around the professor's face. She laughed at the wind, her blizzard collar up, her spare hand struggling to flatten the flaring folds of her dress. At Leonard's corner they said farewell to Goodwin and struggled home up Clanbrassil Street.

Molly was flushed and excited by the wind. Bloom raked over the coals of the fire and fried up some pieces of lap of mutton for her supper. He dished them up with a helping of the Sharwood's Chutney that she loved from Leveret and Frye's. While he watched the meat, he could glance up and see her sitting on the bed, unclasping her stays, which fell with a swish and soft flop on the bed. She came in and sat by the fire, where Bloom unrolled her stockings while she nibbled the chops of mutton with her fingers, dipping the pieces in the chutney. Then he mulled some navy rum and sat sipping it while she removed her hairpins slowly and brushed out her hair. It was after two when Molly made her way to bed and last thing before joining her there, Bloom looked in on the child, to reassure himself of her steady breathing . . . . They were happy then.

That winter Bloom too had been involved with musical matters. Meeting Michael Gunn one day outside the Catholic Apostolic Church (Irvingite) in Adelaide Road, near his residence, Bloom had been asked to write something for *Sinbad the Sailor*, the pantomime which Gunn was presenting at the Gaiety that year.

'It will be a really fine show, Bloom, really fine. All the big names. T.W. Volt, Willie Crackles, F.J. Little, Jess Smith, the Three Ollos, and not least I should tell you, the Great Royce himself.'

'Not Turko the Terrible'.

'The very one. "I am the lad that can..."'

' "... enjoy invisibility." Very good so. What would you like?'

'Something along the lines of "If Brian Boru could but come back and see old Dublin now". The music'll be by Johnson. The book for the show is by Greenley Whither.'

The Blooms, naturally enough, were there when it opened on St Stephen's night. Among other friends they met Simon and May Dedalus with whom they had supper afterwards. They were all enchanted by the Grand Ballet of the Diamonds and the Dance, and by the female transformation scene in which Winter was changed into Summer.

May Dedalus was full of Royce however.

'He'll be appearing in February for a special show. Perhaps we can see it, Simon. Oh, how I remember the opening of the Gaiety, and Royce as Turko the Terrible. It was all too enchanting, so completely unreal and fairy tale. Quite took me out of myself, which is what one wants.'

But Bloom could not deal with the song and it was never performed. This was one of those lost opportunities in life, but a few years later he was asked again by Gunn for another song. That too came to nothing. Literary endeavour was quite beyond Leopold Bloom.

In March 1893 the Blooms moved again, to a flat in Raymond Terrace, a small terrace house further out the Circular Road. There one morning in the late winter light Molly was aroused by the sight of two dogs coupling on the road opposite under the barrack wall.

'Give us a touch, Poldy. God, I'm dying for it.'

And there in that upper room, where they could hear the shouts of the soldiers in the square, they conceived their second child.

Happiness still clung about them. That year Milly, aged four, gave her father a moustache cup, which he long treasured as a memento of her childish love.

There was an outing by the choir to the Sugar Loaf. Scrambling over those loose rocks, Bloom sprained his ankle. Molly was wearing her new elephant grey dress, a lovely thing which fitted her like a glove, even though her fullness with the new baby was fast showing. Molly was livid.

Leopold took to his bed, where Miss Stack from off the South Circular Road would drop in to visit him with flowers (the only man she could find, according to Molly). Molly suspected the visits were merely to provide Miss Stack with entry to a man's bedroom, and she was livid again that Bloom encouraged her.

It was a hot summer that year, so hot that in the drought water had to be drawn from the canal which had been frozen over and skated on in January. Winter into summer: a grand transformation scene was now to involve the Blooms.

Late in 1893, they moved across the city when Bloom took a job with Joe Cuffe the cattleman. They had been happy on Raymond Terrace: now things began to change. On 29 December a son, christened Rudolph, was born. But Rudy was a sickly child and only lived eleven days, dying on 9 January 1894.

The Blooms never recovered from this loss. For Leopold and Molly Bloom ordinary marital intercourse had ceased on Tuesday 27 November 1893. After the death of Rudy it was never resumed. Fearful of another child, they resorted to various forms of birth control. They imported, under plain cover, protectives from London, and Bloom was accustomed to carry one about with him in his wallet. But generally this proved unsatisfactory. Bloom became impotent, at least with his wife. He could not manage the 'trick of the loop', in Dublin parlance.

Molly grew restless and hysterical. Dublin rumour soon suggested they might be thinking of a divorce. But Dublin rumour, especially as relayed by a new acquaintance — Pisser Burke of the City Arms Hotel — was wrong.

1894

Old Bushmills Pure Malt Whiskey. The only Gold Medal Awarded for Whiskey, Paris, 1889. What leading men say about it:—

Professor William K. Sullivan, Queen's College, Cork, says:— "Old Bushmills is one of the choicest specimens of whiskey I ever tasted, and it is free from fusel oil, not in the ordinary analytical sense, but because it passes into ethers."

Duke of Abercorn writes:— "The whiskey will be much appreciated."

Curtis Bros. Electrical Engineers, Opticians, Scientific Instrument Makers. Manufacturers of Electrical, Optical and Photographic Specialities. 10 Suffolk Street, Dublin.

Caterer to H.R.H. Prince Edward of Saxe Weimar and Officers' Mess of the Dublin Garrison. T. Gribbin, Foreman to the late B. Fernback. Respectfully begs to intimate to the public that he has always on hands a supply of the following Goods:— Genuine Pork Sausages and Forced Meats, Limerick Hams and Bacon, Wiltshire Bacon, Sugar-cured Ox Tongues, Fresh and Pickled Pork, Larding Bacon and Pure Lard, Brawn and German Sausages. And can also supply to order the following goods:— Ornamental Boars' Heads, Ornamental Gelatines, Game Pies, Veal and Ham Pies, Small Pork Pies, and Sausage Rolls (Fresh Daily), Spiced Rounds, Glazed Hams, and Tongues. T. Gribbin, 1 & 2 William Street. All above regularly supplied to Sir Charles Cameron and approved of.

J.W. Elvery & Co., Elephant House, Dublin, Cork and Lon-

don. *Established 1850. Waterproofers. Waterproofs for Fishing, Shooting, Riding, Walking. Ladies' Waterproof Cloaks — a speciality. Waterproof Cart and Horse Covers. Mechanical Rubber Dealers. 46, Lower Sackville Street, 18½ Nassau Street, Dublin.*

Killarney Lakes. By Her Most Gracious Majesty's Special Permission. The Royal Victoria Hotel, Patronised by H.R.H. The Prince of Wales; by H.R.H. Duke of Connaught; and by the Royal Families of France and Belgium, etc., the Nobility and Gentry of Great Britain and Ireland, and Leading American Families. Magnificently situated on Lower Lake, facing Inisfallen, open throughout the year. Postal Telegraph Office in the House.

The most complete and choicest selection of poetry ever produced for the use of Young Readers. Now Ready. Small Crown 8vo, 492 pp., cloth, gilt, Price 3s. 6d., *Many Valuable Copyrights; no commonplace or doggerel; all truly Poetical. Suitable for Gift or Prize Book, or for General Home and School Reading.* THE STANDARD READER. *Specimens free to Head Teachers and Managers on application to the Publishers, Alex. Thom & Co. (Limited), 87, 88 & 89 Abbey Street, Dublin.*

Cheap Fuel of the Best Quality. The Alliance and Dublin Consumers' Gas Company Beg to give their Customers and the Public Notice, that they are manufacturing Coke of the Best Quality, from Newcastle Coal, and are now disposing of the same at 12s. per chaldron (ex carriage), also Broken Coke, Suitable for Domestic Use, Hotels, Smithies, Etc., Etc., at 19/6 per ton. A ton being equal to a chaldron and a half of ordinary Coke. Carriage extra. At the Gas Works, Mounttown, Kingstown and Great Brunswick-street, Dublin.

Thomas Dockrell and Sons, & Co., (Limited). Wall Paper Department. Newest Designs on Plain, Coloured, Satin, Embossed, Gilt Japanese, and Imitation Leather Paper; Room and Picture Mouldings.

Central Bank, 22 Fownes's Street, Dublin. This Bank is prepared to make individual advances — £20 to £2,000 on

Notes of Gentlemen, Houses, Lands, Stocks, Shares, Plate, Jewels, Etc. Strong Room provided for the safe-keeping of Valuables. Note:— No connection with Other Discount Houses.

"Knowledge is Power". Explanatory Book (Thirteenth Annual Edition) sent gratis and post free, gives valuable and reliable information how to make money quickly and succesfully by Stocks and Shares. Address:— Geo. Evans & Co., Stockbrokers, 24 Queen Victoria Street, London, E.C.

4

At the City Arms

Bloom's new job was in the city cattle market, and they made their new home in the City Arms Hotel.

The City Arms was a large building, looming over the shops and houses at 55 Prussia Street, just off the North Circular Road, behind the pens and stalls of the cattle market. The Irish Cattle Traders and Stock Owners (Thomas Sherlock, Secretary) had their offices in the building which was a business resort as well as a hostelry for cattlemen. On market days, the bar was the busiest on the North Side.

These bustling premises were presided over by Miss Elizabeth O'Dowd, though she called herself 'Mrs' in the customary manner of landladies. The house had originally been the home of the Jameson family, the famous Dublin distillers, with large orchards behind (on which the market was laid out). It had been enlarged in 1850 by the addition of a third storey.

When the cattle market was opened in 1875, the house became a hotel. The ceiling rondels, painted by Angelica Kaufmann, looked down now on Meath graziers and Connaught drovers.

Bloom was employed as a clerk by Joe Cuffe. The family firm, Lawrence Cuffe and Sons, was long established, dating back in business to the 1840s. Joe Cuffe had succeeded his father in the premises at 5 Smithfield, and in his large fortune. Joe Cuffe was a justice of the peace with a grand mansion on Elgin Road. He also possessed a country place at Cuffesboro, Ballacolla. Cattle trading was then the real wealth of Ireland, and this cattle market was the centre of the developing economy of the country. For Bloom it was a job.

The position required him to be up and about early in

the market. Mornings in the cattle yards with the cows and sheep mooing and maaing in their pens and folds, the cattle-men trudging through the straw and dung, admiring the meaty flanks of the steaming beasts, had a gamey attraction all their own.

Some of the animals went straight into the slaughter house across the road to be poleaxed for the Irish meat market: Friday was slaughtering day. Others were herded off through the streets down along the North Circular Road to the cattle boats moored at the North Wall.

Cattle and men — prime Irish exports. Mr Bloom often contemplated, like other economists before and after him, the loss to Ireland of both brains and brawn. The by-products as well, hair, hides, hooves and such like, might have been utilised in Ireland if so many organising intelligences had not also taken ships to foreign parts.

But if the job had its peculiar features, so had living in an hotel. The water closet was a particular horror. Molly always found someone inside when she wanted to use it, 'leaving their stinks behind them'.

At least once in the month, Bloom would have his break-fast in bed, when he claimed to be assailed with an ill-defined affliction. Laid up with a sick voice, he gave rise to rumours about 'his monthlies'.

Another resident of the hotel was Mrs Riordan, a lady who had lived until recently with Mr and Mrs Simon Dedalus in Martello Terrace, by the sea in Bray. But at Christmas 1891, as she explained to the Blooms, she had fallen out with Mr Dedalus on the vexed question of Parnell and Mrs O'Shea and the bishops.

'He said we were a priest-ridden race, because the people heeded the words of their bishops and rejected that public sinner. I could not have that. I said we should be proud of our priests. God and religion before everything. Well! Then the blackguard banged the table, and shouted "No God for Ireland." Terrible, terrible. I left soon after. Parnell indeed, that devil out of hell. But we won, Mr Bloom, we won.'

In her excitement she failed to notice that Mr Bloom said nothing. But he could not help but feel at one with Simon Dedalus on this matter. The hounds had dragged down a noble stag. Parnell at Bay, the Monarch of the Glen.

Bloom would not have Mrs Riordan think he agreed with such a profane priest-baiter, however. To Mrs Riordan, now old and infirm, Bloom was the model of kindness in the hope that he might be mentioned in her will. Mrs Riordan was close with her cash. Even four pennies for methylated spirits was a burden to her purse.

Mrs Riordan's Skye terrier, like many dogs belonging to old ladies, had peculiar habits. Molly hated the way the creature nosed up the hem of her petticoats. Dogs were dreadful things, she felt, smelly and dangerous. Only the awful gougers from the country who crowded into the hotel on market day — a hopeless race of idiots, she felt — were worse.

In the summer evenings, after supper, Bloom would walk out with Mrs Riordan in her bath chair, from the City Arms Hotel up the hill to the corner of the North Circular Road, where she would quiz the passing traffic and pedestrians with her opera glasses.

Poor Mrs Riordan's stomach rumbled all the time, which was not surprising given the quality of the food in the hotel. The Blooms dined *table d'hote*, a designation covering a simple meal of soup, joint and sweet.

The other guests, too, could easily corner them after eating in the evening. Mrs Duggan was a particular bore. Her husband would roll home drunk, she said, 'the stink of the pub off him as strong as a pole-cat, his stink up your nose all night.' And then in the morning ask, 'Was I drunk last night?' Molly shared her low opinion of men, but Mrs Duggan's stories became too familiar.

A small, but pleasing feature of the hotel which Bloom long remembered was the half tabbywhite tortoise-shell cat with the letter M on its forehead. A multicoloured cat, a mixture of foreign genes and mysterious ways. Bloom liked cats, and would always have one in the house whenever he could. He admired their independence. How different from fawning dogs!

A less pleasant resident of the City Arms was another actuary in the cattle trade called Andrew Burke. To his drinking friends, the familiars of such places as Mulligan's and Barney Kiernan's, he was familiarly known as Pisser Burke. A problem with his prostate put pressure on his bladder which made drinking a matter of frequent trips to the latrine.

Burke was less interested in his work around the cattle market than in gathering gossip about his fellow citizens. Burke was a crony of Simon Dedalus, long a fixture in the rates office and privy to many a household secret. Between them no reputation was safe, no family skeleton unaired. They were malice aforethought incarnate.

Pisser Burke naturally added the Blooms to his collection. His stories in Barney Kiernan's were much enjoyed. He it was that retailed the story of Bloom's 'monthlies', suggesting, of course, that Bloom was 'a quare one' in more than one way, a 'mixed middling'.

But he had other stories. About Bloom and Mrs Riordan's stupid nephew, and how Bloom took him on a monumental round of the city pubs to teach him for once the evils of drink. This laudable enterprise of Christian charity ended in Bloom being roasted by Molly, Mrs O'Dowd and Mrs Riordan. Pisser would imitate poor Bloom's 'but don't you see' when it was plain they didn't. The nephew later got a job in Power's, the whiskey blenders in Cope Street, (less famous than the John's Lane distillery of the same name) and drank his way through the firm's blends, returning footless by cab five days out of seven.

Molly may have resented Mrs Duggan's confidences, but she herself often cried over her husband with Mrs O'Dowd, as Pisser duly related. What Burke did not know, naturally, was the cause of her tears. Bloom's constant questions: would she have sex with a coalman, with a bishop, with the German emperor?

A prize gem was the tale of Bloom taking Molly out in a boat at Bray, despite her inability to swim, and with his careless handling of the boat endangering them both. It was typical.

Bloom was, indeed, inconsiderate, stubborn and pig-headed. He was also a sharp-eyed busybody with a flow of constant chatter. Once on the way to the Mallow Concert where Molly was to sing, he insisted on ordering soup at Maryborough in the station buffet. As the train was about to leave, he then insisted on finishing the soup before he paid, and walked the length of the platform gulping it. He was cheered on by the passengers in the third class, who were amused at the waiter who followed, yelling at him. But Molly was mortified. Then at Mallow he had to force open the carriage door with his knife. Sometimes he could make her miserable with his queer ways.

In those days the Blooms led a hectic social life, a round of theatre and concert going of which the Mallow Concert was only one excursion of many. One even more memorable event was a fund-raising dinner in the Glencree Reformatory in the winter of 1894. This was memorable because it was fixed in Bloom's mind by its association with the great fire in Arnott's of that year, when the whole block between Henry Street and Prince's Street was burned to the ground.

Val Dillon, who was lord mayor of Dublin that year, was one of the principal guests. Molly, indeed, fancied she caught him leering at her décolletage over the dessert nuts thus adding himself to her husband's mythology of men who had been her 'lovers'. The dinner itself was delightful, served on fine china with real silver forks and servers. Molly was rightly impressed.

And there were other 'entertainments', such as Alderman Robert O'Reilly pouring his port into the soup before the flag fell. A man who could not wait until the sun was down, it seemed. With the fearful noise of the guests, the music of the band was quite drowned. Molly was wearing her elephant-grey dress with the braided frogs and silk covered buttons. She looked very smart indeed.

Sir Charles Cameron was there, and Dan Dawson spoke. Bartell D'Arcy (another of Molly's 'lovers') and Benjamin Dollard sang for their suppers. The catering was by Delahunt of Camden Street, and Lenehan the popular sporting journalist was chief steward. There were generous supplies of port and sherry and curacao, with cold joints and mince pies as a supper with which to finish the night.

Afterwards, in the clear winter night, the Blooms and their party drove back into the city in the early morning by way of the Featherbed Mountain. Along with them went Chris Callinan and Lenehan (at that time still writing on racing for *Sport*). While Callinan and Bloom discussed astronomy and tried to identify the stars wheeling above them, Lenehan settled himself beside Molly. There he edged up to her ample figure, making his presence felt, so to speak.

Coming down the mountains they sang glees and duets: *Lo, the early beam of morning*:

> Lo! the early beam of morning
> Softly chides our longer stay
> Hark! the matin bells are chiming,
> Daughter we must haste away.

Lenehan, aside from bouncing against her, was solicitous in settling her boa and tucking in her blanket, his hands passing over her ample charms all the while. Meanwhile the stars in their courses distracted her husband. Bloom knew them all, and repeated their names. Lenehan, hard on, held himself in. Molly, sporting a distant speck, asked: 'And what star is that, Poldy?'

Bloom gazed up in growing doubt. Chris Callinan put her right:

'That one, sure that's only what you might call a pin-prick.' Indeed you might, thought Lenehan.

And so down into the city all covered in snow. It was very late indeed when they arrived at the City Arms. The lights were out, and they were let in by the porter, candle in hand to light them upstairs. Molly had taken his arm as they stepped down from the carriage. In Leopold's veins a faint sense of renewed lust coursed again. There was a fire in their room. But Molly herself was remote in mood and did not answer to his feelings. At last he could bear it no longer.

'Molly dear, what are you thinking about?'

'Oh' she said, after a pause, 'I was thinking about that song.'

'What about the song? Why does it make you sad?'

'I was thinking about a person long ago who used to sing that song.'

'Who was that?' Bloom asked kindly.

'Someone I knew once long ago on Gibraltar.'

He was struck with fear. He knew so little of her past, which must contain much that would have both astonished and distressed him. Molly sat on the bed, half undressed. She slowly began to tell him of the summer when she was only fifteen, but advanced for her age. A British navy lieutenant, named Mulvey, kissed her under the Moorish Wall. Her first kiss, to be remembered to her dying day.

Later, Bloom lay beside her in the dark, gazing at the falling snow in the lamplight, thinking of Gibraltar and how different the nights must be there. Beside him, Molly moved in her sleep, gnashed her teeth. Love's old sweet song.

She had told him little enough. Lieutenant Harry Mulvey was fair haired, with a laughing kind of voice. He referred to everything as 'the whatyoucallit'. He had an elegant moustache too. He promised he would return — and if she were married they would be lovers. She promised she'd let him make love to her. That was only eight years before, so he would have been only in his forties, perhaps a captain, he mused, or an admiral. Or perhaps he was married to some girl in Cappoquin on the Blackwater, where he came from. They had kissed passionately in the open air and then she had pulled him off into her handkerchief. And then they had walked back over the hill through the Jews' cemetary. . . .

Love's old sweet song: in *The Shadow of Ashleydyat*, which Molly had lent him, there was a photo of Mulvey. She left it there for Bloom to find, so that he would know she had not been without admirers. . . .

Love's old sweet song: all her youth he never knew.

1896

Incandescent Gas Light (Walsbach Patents). Further Reductions in Prices Due to Colossal Sales, Places this Highly Popular Light Within the Means of all Classes. The Greatly Reduced Consumption of Gas Covers the Initial Cost of the Burners in from 6 to 8 months. 50% Saving on Gas Bills. The Prices have been Reduced as follows:—

The Ordinary "C" Burner 6 —   — Price   9/-
The "C" By-Pass Burner   —   — Price 11/-

The Light of Ireland. For further Particulars apply to The Irish Incandescent Gas Light Co., Ltd., 62 Grafton Street, Dublin.

Established 1840. John Smyth & Sons, 17 Wicklow-street, Dublin. Medieval & Italian Metal Workers in Gold and Silver. Electro Platers and Gilders. Brass for Ecclesiastical and Domestic Purposes. Special Drawings Made. Architects' Drawings estimated for.

Mrs H. Glenville, Theatrical and General Costumier, 36 Marlborough Street, Dublin. Scenerey and Costumes made to Order. For Sale or Hire. Every Requisite for Amateurs.

Murray & Co., Umbrellas, Corsets, and Walking Sticks, 13 St Andrew Street, Dublin. Largest Finishers of Irish Blackthorn Walking Sticks.

The Irish Portland Cement & Brick Company, Limited. First Lock Works, Grand Canal, Dublin. These Works having been entirely remodelled and provided with machinery of the most modern type, the company is now in a position to supply

Portland Cement of the highest quality at lowest rates. Medal and Highest Award, Chicago, 1893.

Royal Marine Hotel, Kingstown. The Magnificent Hotel, unrivalled in situation, opposite the Royal Mail Packet Pier, and commanding extensive view of Dublin Bay, is now being made up to date by the addition of Electric Light.
Electric Light. Hot and Cold Salt Water Baths. High-Class Cuisine. Very Moderate Charges. Table D'Hote 3s. 6d.

Stained Glass Establishment. J. Andersen & Son, 107 Lower Gloucester Street, Dublin. Most Recent Works Executed: St Michael's, Kingstown.

Cantrell & Cochrane's 31 Gold and Prize Medal Table Waters. Bottled Under Pressure at the Well of St Patrick, St Patrick's Well Lane, Nassau Place, Dublin, Ireland. The Countess of Aberdeen has made arrangements with Messrs Cantrell and Cochrane for the sole supply of their "Club Soda" at the Irish Village refreshment stalls, World's Fair, Chicago.

John F. Clarke, Forage Contractor and Coal Importer, office 11 Upper Ormond Quay, Dublin. Horse Carrots, Pickled Table Potatoes & all other Farm Produce sold in quantities to customers, at the Lowest Market Price.

M'Glade faithfully carries out contracts. M'Glade gives satisfaction to his clients.
B. M'Glade, Bill Poster, Advertising Contractor, and Artistic Sign and Poster Writer, 2 Chapel Lane (off Great Britain Street), Dublin. Street Advertising Vans at the Lowest City Prices.

Tailoring. William Gunn begs to inform his Customers that he has now his Autumn and Winter Goods in. Gentlemen's own materials made up on the premises. 2 Fownes Street, Upper (Dame Street).

Irish Poplins for Vestments as Woven for Maynooth College. Satins and Figured Silks in All Church Colours. Special designs woven to order. Thomas Elliott, Manufacturers, 25 Brown Street, Weavers Square, Dublin.

5

The Wandering Years

Bloom, ever the pigheaded one, was eventually fired by Joe Cuffe for insulting a grazier. Molly made desperate efforts to have him re-employed, but Cuffe was adamant.

'It's no use pleading, Mrs Bloom, I can't have him back.' She shifted in her chair, and he eyed her bosom with interest. 'The business depends on friendly good will. I can't have my clerks giving cheek to the cattlemen. Can't be done.'

With no job in the cattle market, they could not stay on in the City Arms Hotel. So, while Bloom hunted round for another job and was eventually taken back by Wisdom Hely, Molly had to be content to make a new home for them in Holles Street, where they had taken a furnished apartment.

His friends were later to refer to Bloom, contemptuously, 'as a traveller in blotting paper'. And that essential article of office material was one of the items he carried. But Hely did whole ranges of stationary, office supplies, and printing work. Bloom's job was to sell these and to have old contracts renewed more favourably, mostly around the city of Dublin. Another part of the job was the collection of overdue accounts. As some of these were owed by religious orders they could not politely be referred to as 'bad debts'.

Among these were the Carmelite nuns in the Tranquilla Convent in Upper Rathmines. The good sisters were an enclosed contemplative order who prayed for the world. Bloom, calling one morning about the account, talked to a nice nun, with a sweet face whom he took away from her morning devotions. She was the daughter of Patrick Claffey, the pawnbroker in Amiens Street.

'About the account, Sister.'

'Ah, this you know is our great day — 16 July — the feast of Our Lady of Mount Carmel.'

'Indeed sister. Now.'

'But we must return to worldly things, of course. We have so little money Mr Bloom. So little money.'

But their breakfast was fried in best butter, as he could smell. She told him of a girl who had a strange longing, she liked to sniff rock oil. Very strange. Some cheap papers smelled of rock oil. They agreed on the strange tastes of young girls. Her name in religion was Sister Agatha, and on another visit they spoke of the apparitions of Mount Carmel, Knock and Lourdes. (In 1920 Bloom was to recall this in the excitement over the bleeding statue at Templemore.) The soft face, the remote eyes, the ethereal nature of her spirit, the white habit coif and winged wimple, deeply impressed the spiritual side of Bloom's nature.

The debts of the world seemed sometimes a small thing beside the wealth of the spirit. His own debts were also a difficulty. While in the City Arms he had been in a card game one evening with Pisser Burke and a few others. He explained that Milly was sick, and Molly called down a speaking tube about her progress so Bloom at an appointed moment could vamoose with his winnings. This was thought unsporting of him.

Milly was, however, a healthy enough child. She had mumps, of course, worms, measles. She got flaxseed tea for that one. But she also contracted wildfire and nettle-rash, for which she was given a calomel purge.

She was her father's joy: she would put her small hand into his as they went among the shops, and sit on his lap counting his waistcoat buttons. She had called herself Padney Socks as a child: now she was Silly Milly. She had a doll, a sailor boy, *HMS Invincible* on his cap.

When he thought of her later in life memories crowded in: a hoop, a skipping rope flung in a corner. He tied her hair ribbon while she bent forward that delicate, vulnerable arch of neck. Leaning over the bridge in Stephen's Green she spat gently down into the lake to show him where a sleeping fish lay. In 1893 she gave him a breakfast moustache cup of imitation Crown Derby — long treasured. He told her about Plevna, so famous in his father-in-law's mind, and she pulled her plait to remember it. She said that she wished she had a quarter or a thousandth of his knowledge.

'Oh daddy, you are so clever.'

She told him her own story of the horse named Joseph who drank lemonade. He kept her drawings and baby letters. She was too imaginative though. Once in Crumlin Molly persuaded him to hide behind a tree. Milly felt she had lost them suddenly, and burst into tears. 'Mamma, Mamma, where are you?' However on an excursion from the North Wall on the *Erin's King* around the Kish lighthouse on a rough day she showed no fear at all. She stood resolute with her pale blue scarf flowing back behind her in the wind. He threw stale cake out to the screaming gulls and she squinted up into the sun to see them. Others on board were sick, vomiting over the side. Youth was resilient, but then children have no fear, and clean stomachs unsullied by drink. The smoke from the ship's stack was caught up by the wind and blown away. Happy days they had been.

But Bloom was soon fired by Wisdom Hely, and their life dipped to the nadir. In Holles Street, as Molly later recalled, they were 'on the rocks'. This was in 1895 and late Victorian Dublin was not an easy place to be 'on the rocks'.

Holles Street was a short and not very distinguished street running down from Merrion Square into Denzille Street. At the Merrion Square end, the imposing facade of the National Maternity Hospital dominated all around it.

Much of the street, except for the tenements at the lower end, and a private hotel, was let out in furnished lodgings. Such was the Blooms' flat, in a house owned by a Nurse Callan. The windows overlooked the hospital directly.

Money was desperately short. Bloom seemed at this time incapable of holding down a job. Some devil would get into him, he would come out with some unwanted advice or un- called for witticism, and he would be fired. His attitude to his employers was never cowering enough. He was always ready with a good excuse or a smart remark. One too many, even with patient men like Cuffe and Hely, often meant the loss of yet another job, another wage packet, and another row with Molly.

With her husband often idle, Molly had to resort to other ways of earning some ready cash. She began by selling some of her clothes. But they did not last for long. She then took a

65

job playing the piano in the Coffee Palace in Townsend Street, even though this did not pay her very much. There were tips, as well, of course. For now she had a new circle of admirers for her pretty voice and full figure. Soon enough she was to be something more than a mere attraction to them.

Bloom had suggested she might pose in the nude for an artist or a student in the College of Art, over in Kildare Street. But Molly had hopes of more than that. Eventually she did pose, but for a sculptor named John Hughes, a strangely amusing little man associated with the College of Art. He was a real sculptor, she would explain, not a mere purveyor of church decorations like some of those fellows down in Townsend Street or Brunswick Street. A real artist, she always emphasised.

He was working on a Madonna for a church in the West of Ireland. This was to have a special place in the church. But he could not begin the final shape of his idea until he had the basic form right.

'I would like you to pose for me in the nude please,' indicating a screen in the corner.

'But I thought this was a holy statue.'

'Statues are not holy or unholy. They are works of art. I need to know the flesh beneath the clothes before I can begin.'

And so for several weeks Molly posed in that underheated studio while the sculptor struggled with his design. For the money she was paid, she did not consider it much fun. As she told Leopold later, 'I don't think he ever saw me as a woman. Artists are an oversold article if you ask me.'

At this time she had her photograph taken by Lafayette in Westmoreland Street to circulate as an available model. Molly was vain about the photo, and Bloom himself carried a copy which he often produced for the admiration of strangers.

'My wife you know, Madame Bloom the singer. A good likeness.'

She appeared to more critical eyes as a large lady with too much of her fleshy appeal on display, in a low cut evening dress posed beside a piano on which lay open the music of that now forgotten song 'In Old Madrid'. Her full lips parted to show perfect teeth, her dark eyes full of promise: it was in its own way a supremely vulgar little production.

The circulation of this print brought her a certain notoriety. Indeed it was said that for a time she was little more than an expensive *demi-mondaine*. Later this era would be a period they did not like to remember. A certain shame covered the nakedness of this economic necessity.

The curiosity of others in the Blooms was echoed by their interest in the relationship between Nurse Callan and the young Dr O'Hare in the hospital opposite. Staying at home so much while Molly was out working, Bloom's mind conjured with this couple. They fitted into the imaginings of his 'secret life' quite well, as we shall see.

Molly herself found that at a performance of Beerbohm Tree's *Trilby* at the Gaiety on 10 October 1895 some fellow in the pit was pushing up against her, touching her behind. A little later she saw him outside Switzer's window trying to get near stylishly dressed ladies.

That winter was a fierce one, marked in Bloom's memory by the sinking of the *Palme*, a Finnish ship. She ran aground on 24 December and a lifeboat was overturned in the rescue, drowning fifteen of the crew. This was the topic of a poem by Albert William Quill, 'The Storm of Christmas Eve 1895'.

That winter too Milly had a bad nightmare, and had to be comforted by both Molly and her father.

Money being short again Bloom resorted to selling Molly's combings, though he only received some ten shillings for them. But as Molly herself did not make much at the Coffee Palace, all cash was welcome.

In the middle of this black period in their lives, Ben Dollard arrived with Bob Cowley and Simon Dedalus to borrow a dress suit for Ben to wear while singing in a concert. It was to be an expensive affair, with five shilling reserved seats. The trousers, however, were a little tight around Ben's scrotum, which doubtless contributed to the pitch of his voice. Molly was delighted.

'Hoho, with all his belongings on show', she cried, kicking on the bed. 'O Saints above, I'm drenched. O, the women in the front row. O, I never laughed so much.'

Their visitors had been surprised, knowing that the Blooms were 'on the rocks', at Molly having so many fine clothes. Simon Dedalus was convinced 'the daughter of the regiment', as he called her, was 'doing the other business'.

The Blooms may have hoped that a legacy would solve their problems. They had visited Mrs Riordan in Our Lady's Hospice for the Dying in Harold's Cross. The terrible appearance of her altered features, the nurse trying to feed her with cup and spoon, dismayed them. But she had turned against them, having heard of Bloom's falling out and Molly's new pursuit. She tore up her will.

'I'm disappointed in you! You bad man!' She left them nothing: all her money went on masses for the dead. This was in 1896. On 21 March that year at 4.46 a.m. the clock that Matt Dillon had given them as a wedding present stopped for ever. This curious event seemed in retrospect to mark off a distinct part of their life. Things could never be so bad again.

Soon after this at the end of that summer, the Blooms moved again, this time to 1 Ontario Terrace, a short row of houses beside the Grand Canal, on the Rathmines side of Charlemont Bridge. As Bloom had now found a position with Alexander Drimmie, the insurance agents in Sackville Street (a penny tram ride from the bridge) they could again afford some comforts, such as a servant girl, Mary O'Driscoll, and oysters from Mr Davy on Charlemont Mall at 2/1d. a dozen.

Bloom was enamoured of the girl, whom Molly considered little better than a slut. She was with them for four months (at £6 per year) with Fridays off. Bloom presented her with a pair of smart emerald green garters. When Christmas came he suggested to Molly that Mary might share their Christmas dinner. But Molly would not have that. She suspected Mary of padding out her bottom to attract the attentions of Leopold. She suspected him too: having found him lurking in the rear premises claiming that he was looking for a glass of water. Later Molly suspected that she stole oysters and potatoes to take to her aunt's house on her day off. Bloom stuck up for the girl.

Naturally enough he did fancy her. So, one morning while Molly was out shopping in Charlemont Street, he made his way down stairs with a request for a safety pin and surprised Mary in 'the rear premises' by clutching her bottom. Mary O'Driscoll beat him off with her scouring brush. Bloom, in his ripplecloth housejacket, flannel trousers, and heelless slippers was put to flight. She claimed he had held her so tight that she was bruised in four places. Twice more he attempted to interfere with her clothing — Bloom felt free as she had been giving him the glad eye. Nothing came of all this, and soon enough the suspicious Molly fired the girl. If it wern't for the cooking and slopping out, she would not have a servant in the house.

Bloom had perhaps a natural sympathy with the lame dogs of life, from Mary to the dog with the sore paw he brought home one night to Ontario Terrace. Such sympathy extended to Milly when (aged eight) she had another memorable nightmare. And for Molly, too, Bloom was a comfort in a crisis. As when, in October 1897, they went to *The Wife of Scarli*, a new play adapted from the Italian original. They shared a box that night with the owner of the theatre, Michael Gunn. It was reputed to be a fast play and from the gallery hissing protesters greeted every appearance of the adultress. Molly's period came upon her in this public situation, much to her mortification. Bloom had helped Gunn over some insurance policies taken out through Drimmies: her embarrassment could cost them money. In the interval, Bloom was telling her about the life and death of Spinoza (all out of a book of his father's, *Thoughts from Spinoza*, which he had inherited). She wore her crocus dress, with its low-cut neckline, and drew admiring glances from a gentleman in the dress circle with opera glasses (lecherous leers Molly thought they were). But once aware of her problem, Bloom spirited her away, down the backstairs to the side entrance. On the way home in the cab, he was a model of kindness.

Drimmies was a good job where Bloom was busy. Once after a row, when Mary O'Driscoll was dismissed, he went to work without a necktie on, an extraordinary lapse, which was commented on.

Bloom was now keen on improving himself and his appearance. At the beginning of May 1899 he attended at the Empire Palace a performance of his skills by Eugene Sandow. The year before Sandow had published in London his book *Strength and How to Obtain It*. Impressed by the performance, Bloom purchased the book and began the course of exercises recommended by Sandow. (Sandow had leapt to fame by challenging Samson, a leading strongman, from the theatre audience on 2 November 1889. His real name was Frederick Muller.) For two months Bloom followed the exercises, noting his measurements before and after on a special chart that came in the book. Body building was all the rage: *mens sana in corpore sano.*

It was while living in Ontario Terace that Bloom attempted an experiment. Before paying it over the counter to Mr Davy, his grocer, Bloom scored the edge of a florin in three places. He wanted to see if it would return to him in the course of time through countless pockets. It never did. Change in nature never allows one the same experience again, or the use of the same coin twice.

The Boer War broke out in 1899. The confrontation of the British and Dutch settlers in South Africa was of long standing. Many Irish people in South Africa tended to side with the Boers, whom they saw as much like the Irish: a nation of small farmers harassed by imperial menaces. That the Boers in their turn regarded the Bantu as an inferior breed did not trouble the Irish. They would have thought nothing of knocking niggers around with a knobkerrie.

When war came in October 1899, after an insolent ultimatum from the Boers followed by the invasion of Natal, it was greeted with enthusiasm by many in Ireland — as well as in Britain. Though the Transvaal and Orange Free State were annexed in 1900, the Boers did not finally surrender until 1902. This was the first conflict of any significance involving British troops since the Crimean War and the Indian Mutiny. Entered into with imperial pride, it marked, in fact, the beginning of the end.

At a personal level, the war came home to Ireland in many ways. Leopold Bloom was pro-Boer, but there was also the matter of his investments, his money tied up in consols, 'his four per cents'. When the war went badly, as it often did, Bloom's pocket suffered.

Then in November he heard the sad news that his old and loved school friend Percy Apjohn had been killed at the battle of Modder River.

The next month Trinity awarded an honorary degree to Joseph Chamberlain, the Colonial Secretary, which he came over to Dublin to receive. There were, inevitably, demonstrations, as he was held responsible for the war. He was also remembered as one of those defecting Liberals whose votes had defeated Parnell's Home Rule Bill in 1886. On 18 December 1899 there were riots by students in the streets. Bloom became involved with a party of medicals, and was chased down Abbey Street by the police. But in this melee he encountered young Dr Dixon as they ducked into Manning's public house to escape the flaying batons.

'Up the Boers'.

'Three cheers for De Wet'.

'We'll hang Joe Chamberlain from a sour apple tree'.

The shriek of the police whistles, the scarpering students, the scream of the protesters: it was vivid and exciting. The British defeats, the exploits of the Irish Brigades fighting with the Boers, the concentration camps for Boer women and children, were later followed by British victories (Mafeking, Ladysmith, Bloemfontein), the deeds of the Royal Dublin Fusiliers at Tugela River, the final defeat of the mounted commandos. Typically 'the relief of Lady Smith', doubtless due to 'Wondermaker' the miracle enema, was a long remembered joke.

Out in South Africa, the Mayoman John MacBride led an Irish Brigade which fought in the field with the Boer commandos; at home Maude Gonne and other extreme nationalists led the opposition to the war in rallies and protests – but despite nationalist enthusiasm for the Boers, a great many Irish people took genuine pride in the achievements of Irish regiments in the British army.

But while Leopold, along with much of Dublin, was bound up in the continuous excitements of the war, Molly was otherwise engaged. At a concert one evening she made the acquaintance of a Lieutenant Stanley G. Gardner. He was very English. At first, indeed, she was afraid he might find her accent too provincial. But Stanley was not a snob, though he did not think much of the young ladies of Dublin. Or of how they sang. Now Molly was different, and so, she thought, was he. Having first seen her in the full flight of song, he was 'dead gone' on her lips.

He asked could he see her and she had little reluctance. While Bloom went about his business on the North Side

71

selling insurance, Molly would take the tram over to Ballsbridge (how well named she thought) to walk with Gardner in the open fields beside the Dodder. At first she was firm. She would touch his trousers outside with her ring hand (as she had once done with Bloom) 'to keep him from doing worse where it was too public'. Bloom, however, could never embrace as well as Gardner could. His arms around her, lips to lips she melted. She gave him Mulvey's claddagh ring with its heavy hands grasped in union: a keepsake of their own grasping union. With his clean shaven face, he was a lovely fellow in his khaki and just the right height over her.

The night before he left they walked along the canal bank and he said she was lovely. He was pale with excitement, and she was hot with lust. They could be seen from the road. She didn't care. The cold brick against her back, the hot weight of his body against her, the hard thrust of him rising within her.

Then he was off to South Africa to join the other units of the East Lancashire Regiment. In that war some 5,000 soldiers were killed in action, but over 16,000 died of wounds or disease. At Bloemfontein (which Lord Roberts, 'Bobs', had occupied on 13 March 1900) Gardner, Lieut Stanley G., 3 Batt. 2 East Lancashire Regiment, died of enteric fever. Molly was upset: a fine looking man and a brave soldier to die that way. Ever after she hated politics, thinking it only another name for sundered loves and blighted lives.

On 5 May 1904 Leopold and Molly were among the large crowd when the Arch of Triumph memorial to the South African dead at the Grafton Street corner of Stephen's Green was dedicated by His Royal Highness, the Duke of Connaught. They had their separate and distinct memories aroused by this ceremony: of the lost days of boyhood, the lost nights of love, despoiled by the grime of war, the pain of disease. The opposite of war, love, was what life ought to be about.

1902

Crow & Williams — attorneys-at-law — General Law Practice, Probate and Corporation Law Specialists. Spokane, Washington. Refer to Exchange National Bank of Spokane.

Thomas Henshaw & Co., Ltd., Wholesale House Furnishings and Manufacturing Ironmongers. Every description of Iron Work. 4, 5, 6, 12, Christ Church Place, Dublin.

The Globe Express, Ltd., Established 1837. Best, Cheapest, & Safest Conveyance for parcels & goods of every description to all Parts of the World. Dublin Offices — 8 Eden Quay.

The Red Guide. A Monthly Guide to Irish Railways, Steamers, Tramways, Etc. Price Twopence. First-class advertising medium.

The Parisian Typewriting & Scrivenry Depot, 30 Upper Ormond Quay, Dublin. Scrivenry, Typewriting, Translations. Maps traced. Neatness, Promptness and Accuracy. Country Orders promptly attended to. Telephone 1523.

The Irish Constable's Guide, By Sir Andrew Reed, K.C.B., Barrister-at-Law, late Inspector-General of Royal Irish Constabulary. Fourth edition: revised and enlarged.
The Liquor Licensing Laws of Ireland and Inn-Keepers Guide, by Sir Andrew Reed, K.C.B., Barrister-at-Law, late Inspector-General of Royal Irish Constabulary.
Dublin: Alex. Thom & Co., Ltd., 87, 88, 89, Abbey Street.

Joseph Kelly & Sons, "The City Saw Mills", 66 and 67

Thomas Street, Dublin. Timber, Slates, and Cement Merchants. Makers of all kinds of Joinery Work. Church Fittings and Ship Fittings our Speciality. Telephone 145.

The Automatic Cyclostyle will Reproduce 1,000 copies from one original handwriting, typewriting, drawing or music. The latest and best machine for printing circulars, price lists, market reports, specifications, returns, and balance sheets, freight lists, manifests, B/L, examination papers, menus, programmes, etc., etc. The Automatic Cyclostyle, price complete, for reproducting handwriting: Octavo size, £3 10s.; Foolscap size, £5; Outfit of Materials for Reproducing Typewriting, 12s. 6d. extra each machine.

John J. Martin. Tallow, Oil & Grease Refiner. Butchers' Fat and Bones Bought. Also every description of Grease and all kinds of stuffs suitable for rendering. Bellevue Works, Bellevue, near James's St Harbour, Dublin. Maker of M Brand of Tallow. Exporter of Bones for Knife Handles.

6

Bloom of the Freeman

In 1901 the new century (as some reckoned it) was marked by the appearance of a nova — as Bloom's own birth had been. But this heralded a death: the demise of Queen Victoria. So long had she reigned that the Victorian era seemed to encompass all of recorded history. For some of the Irish she was 'the Famine Queen', because her own first visit to Ireland came in August 1849, at the end of that fateful visitation of God. With the arrival of Edward, long a notorious rake, a talent wasted, a new era of light-hearted fun and serious doings was ushered in. Stories were widely told about the private life of the new king. The old queen had carried haemophilia — the new king might carry something worse. Not that the queen had been backward in medical matters: she took chloroform, 'twilight sleep', at the birth of Leopold in 1853 (he it was who died of haemophilia). Public interest during her long widowhood was sustained by spirited public gossip about the 'Empress Brown'.

It was a year when the census was taken — the population of the country was now some 4,386,035. On Christmas Day this was reduced by at least one, with the death in Anglesey of Dr O'Hare, Nurse Callan's lover, of cancer.

Gossip exercised itself on lesser mortals than kings. In 1902 it was concerned with Jack Power and his mistress, a barmaid in the Moira, or Jury's — both central hotels. Was there any truth in this, or in the rumour that he would bring her a pound of steak, their appetites being something less than directly carnal?

For the Blooms the new century brought a new address when they moved into 7 Eccles Street. For Bloom this also meant a new position in the *Freeman's Journal*. Now for the first time they had a complete house to themselves, and they relished it. This new house and position gave them the confidence of renewed security and, while domestic life continued as before, they both broadened the range of their social lives.

Eccles Street had seen better days. At the top, opposite the open space before the church, loomed the great bulk of the Mater Hospital. A little nearer was the Dominican Convent, over whose quiet and well-behaved girls Mr Bloom allowed his lustful eye to wander. The houses were not in quite the condition they could have been, but they were still, in those days, in good repair. (Nelson Street, which ran off Eccles Street, was later to be celebrated as the site of the brothel in which a young English soldier was held by the IRA — an incident which suggested *The Hostage* to Brendan Behan.)

The Blooms' house was at the Dorset Street end and got the sun on the front, warming the brown bricks. It was perhaps too large for them — a basement, a ground floor, and two floors about that. They used only the basement and the ground floor, the rest being intended for apartments. A notice to this effect was hung in the window shortly after their arrival.

They had taken the house because Bloom's new position enabled them to do so, but the extra money would be welcome. He had hoped they might make a lodging house of it. But Molly was not anxious for the work, or for giving Milly the run of the lodgers, who would all be clerks or what have you.

Bloom's position on the *Freeman* required him to scout out and obtain advertisements for the paper on long-term contracts. Though he was paid a retainer, much of what he earned was by way of commission. He had a vested interest in placing the ads, and would often go to great trouble to set them up correctly and to satisfy the personal whims of the clients. Without Bloom's labours there might have been no *Freeman's Journal* to grace the morning table of those Dublin homes where the *Irish Times* would never gain admittance. The journalistic world of Dublin was a small one, the journalists themselves moving easily from paper to .paper. And there were then a great many of them: *Freeman's Journal, Irish Times, Daily Express, Evening Herald, Evening Telegraph* and, oldest of them all, *Evening Mail* (once owned by Sheridan le Fanu). As well as these there were sporting journals, Catholic papers, and social journals. The vivid, varied round of pleasure, news and business.

Bloom was, of course, on the edge of all of this, somewhat scorned by the scribblers. Naturally enough, he harboured literary ambitions. Hoping to begin at an easy level, he planned to contribute stories to *Titbits*. By degrees he might mount the scale. He could in the end become an Edgar Wallace, or a William Le Queux. He imagined it all: Germans menace Ireland, hero saves the day. But though he actually prepared a manuscript and sent it out, it never was published. And the literary remains of Leopold Bloom remained that, remains.

Aside from the journalists there were a few others in this field due for better things. Men like Gabriel Conroy, who wrote for the *Express* and Stephen Dedalus whose poems and stories appeared in magazines and journals such as the *Irish Homestead*. And then there were those for whom the papers were a means to an end, usually a political end. Chief among these was Arthur Griffith.

It was during the Boer War that Dublin became aware of Arthur Griffith. He was a friend of Maud Gonne, the fiery woman leader of the extreme nationalists, and of John MacBride, the hard-drinking leading of an Irish pro-Boer unit against the British. Arthur Griffith had lived in South Africa — he knew the Boers and the British, admired the Boers and hated the British. Through his newspapers Griffith called for a re-alignment in Irish politics. He was a familiar figure in the streets, in the National Library and in the Bailey, taking a stout and a cheese sandwich before going home to his house in Summerhill. His office in Fownes Street (between Dame Street and Temple Bar) was the haunt of many on the radical fringe of Irish life and politics.

Bloom's meeting with Griffith (though not recorded in conventional lives of Griffith) was accidental but of mementous consequence. Early one evening in July 1902, Bloom had drifted into the Bailey. It was early; there was no crowd.

As Bloom was waiting for his drink, a glass of wine, to go with a sandwich, a new customer drifted up beside him and, after ordering his drink, began to discuss with the barman the ructions in the Austro-Hungarian Empire.

'Excuse me', said Bloom, 'but this interests me greatly, being as you might say, Hungarian myself.'

'Indeed, how interesting. My name is Griffith, Arthur Griffith. You may have heard of me. I run a small newspaper. Come over into the corner to that free table and tell me about Hungary.'

'My name is Bloom, Leopold Bloom. I'm with your rival,' he said, 'the *Freeman's Journal.*'

'Ah yes,' said Griffith. 'Well, we will talk only of the freeman's bloom — Hungarian liberty.'

Bloom explained how his father had left Hungary and how he had finally come to Dublin in 1865.

'That would have been before the events of 1867,' said Griffith.

'That is so but of course my father knew all about Deák and Kossuth and 1848. That was a year of rebellion in Hungary as well as in Ireland.'

'Ah, but Ireland failed and Hungary didn't. How was that?'

'Because we put away this childishness of revolutionary cliques. True progress can only be made by the people themselves. Constitutional agitation, carrying the people's opinion, that is what won the day for Hungary. The crowning of Franz Joseph as King of Hungary in 1867 was the result. We could do that here.'

'Perhaps we could', mused Griffith, intrigued. 'Of course, O'Connell half-attempted something similar in '43.'

Bloom sat on the edge of his seat, now talking quickly.

'Imagine Edward crowned King of Ireland — a separate kingdom — a dual monarchy with our own parliament. Wonderful, wouldn't it be? The end of years of struggle.'

'We must talk more about this', said Griffith when he rose to leave. His home was out in Summerhill and Mr Bloom walked back across the city with him. And as they walked a new scheme formed in Griffith's mind. Impressed by Bloom's account, he would try to develop the Hungarian experience as a model for Ireland. In October he first formulated the 'Hungarian model' in public and all through 1903 he sought to elaborate it in his own mind. In the first six months of 1904, he wrote a series of articles for his newspaper on the subject. Towards the end of that year, these twenty-seven articles were collected and issued in book form, under the title *The Resurrection of Hungary*. In 1905, he founded a new political grouping, Sinn Fein, which had the 'Hungarian model' as a central policy plank.

When he died suddenly seventeen years later, Arthur Griffith was President of the Dail, the newly-independent Irish parliament. He was the first Irish leader to be buried as a head of state.

1904

Why Pay Rent? When you may become your own landlord by joining the National Benefit Trust, Ltd., 13 Dame Street, Dublin. Advantages unsurpassed by any other Society are offered its Members to secure their own houses by paying less than Rent. Interest allowed from 3 to 4½ per cent.

Begley and Sons, Van, Carriage and Wheel Builders. Wheels Repaired and Shod Daily. Rubber Tyres of all Patterns. All Our Work Guaranteed. Spare Vehicles Lent. Telephone 02277. Works 5 to 12 Harmony Row, Dublin.

The Bernard—"Mnemo-Imprest" System of Perfect Double Entry. Book-keeping and Forms of Accounts for Creameries, Dairies, Drapers, Engineers, Factors, Grocers, and General Trade and Merchants, Etc.
A chart of this "B-M-I" System of Double Entry Book-keeping for any Trade, Whole-sale or Retail, will be Ready in and after January 1904, sent on application to D. Bell, A.C.I.S., Publisher, of 3, Lower Merrion Street, Dublin.

Ask for "Kandee" (The New Irish Sauce). Appetizing, Delicious, Digestive. Price 2d. and 4½d. per Bottle. Sold everywhere. Annual sales exceed one million bottles.

Cummins and Sons, Electrical Engineers & Contractors for Electric Light Installations, Telephones, and Electric Bells. Hot and Cold Water Fittings. Sanitary Works and Gas Fittings. Estd. 1867. 10 and 12 Lower Abbey Street, Dublin.

George Prescott & Son, 9 Merrion Row, Dublin. Maker of

7

The Pattern of Life

Courtship, marriage, children: these are the things of youth. But when one's friends first begin to die, intimations of old age set in, even if one is only thirty-seven.

In October 1903 Bloom was distressed to read in the evening paper of the death of Mrs Emily Sinico, of Leoville, Sydney Parade. She had attempted to cross the Dublin-Wexford railway line at Sydney Parade station while drunk and had been hit by the train from Kingstown. He had got to know Captain and Mrs Sinico because they were neighbours of the Helys and later of the Drimmies at Linwood on the other end of the Parade. He had met her at several small gatherings, and later he and Molly sometimes encountered her at concerts, either with her daughter or in the company of a gentleman friend whom she introduced as Mr Duffy. He was a reserved, bespectacled creature who made little impression upon one.

Mr Bloom went to the funeral in Glasnevin. There he heard the whole sad story. In her last months she had taken to drinking heavily. It had been suggested at the time that there had been some unpleasantness in her life of late. But at the inquest this had not been inquired into. The verdict had been one of misadventure. Drimmie was there, as well as Wisdom Hely. Both inquired how he was getting on in his new job at the *Freeman's Journal*. There had been other familiar faces from the small Dublin worlds of music and business. But among the group gathered round the grave in Glasnevin he did not see Mr Duffy. Bloom surmised that he had contributed a little to her unhappiness. Mrs Sinico, he suspected, had been a passionate woman, and Duffy had looked like a cold fish. The poor woman had evidently found little comfort in her husband after twenty-two years of marriage. So she had turned elsewhere. A man would have; he couldn't blame a woman if she followed her nature as well.

He felt himself strangely affected by her death. Sydney Parade was an odd place for Bloom. He had always considered it a strange conjunction of fates that two of his late employers should have lived in the same house, Linwood, on the same road. Now Mrs Sinico's death had taken place near the same spot. Life had perhaps some secret design, as the Masons always claimed, if such things were possible. What, he wondered, was the secret design of his life?

It was a brisk cold day, and coming back into town he stepped into a public house and drank three whiskies: a thing he never did usually. He felt the effect of them all day, and regretted his foolishness. He had begun to sense that life was no longer concerned with growth, but decay.

By 1904 the Blooms had been in Eccles Street for two years, and seemed likely to be settled there for some time to come. This year and its events are not of special significance for Leopold, yet in their even tenor the encounters and experiences of that year, like Mrs Sinico's funeral, brought the past into focus with the expectations of the future. On 17 October 1903 he had placed in the pocket of his dress waistcoat a silver shilling, which he only discovered when he next went to a funeral, on 16 June 1904. The past seemed always to be carried in one's pocket to surprise one by its appearance in the future.

Bloom was midway in the path of life. He and Molly had been married for sixteen years. Dubliners had been gossiping about the possibility of Leopold and Marion seeking a separation or divorce. But divorce was still looked upon as an unusual course in Dublin. Whatever choppy waters a couple hit, the ship of marriage usually stayed on course. Character was often the key, and by 1904 the characters of Mr Bloom and his wife had evolved into a set of complex contradictions, between their public lives and private selves.

Mr Bloom's appearance epitomised the public man. Though he possessed a dark suit (worn for funerals), Mr

Bloom preferred suits of a light colour, which had the advantage of reflecting the heat. His thick legs had the appearance of a wading bird's, slightly ludicrous when viewed from the rear. His brown brilliantined hair grew on the long side and came slightly over his collar. His nails were always well pared, however. An athlete in his youth, his body was now a little soft, but the shape was still there: a fine figure of a man. His sad face and dark eyes gave his face some interest — though he was ashamed of his profile, thinking it ugly, and wondering what Molly (or any other woman) could see in it. Like most men, he carried round a miscellany of objects in his pockets: match books, a potato against the rheumatics, a bar of soap and so on. His collar size (please note) was 17. He had taken a course of Eugene Sandow's Sandow-Whiteley pulley chart exerciser. This had come with a form which he had filled up at the beginning: chest 28 and 29½ inches; biceps 9 inches and 10 inches; forearms 8½ and 9 inches; thigh 10 inches and 12 inches; calf 11 inches and 12 inches. He weighed eleven stone and four pounds, stood 5ft 9½ inches, full build and olive complexion. A handsome youth, he had modelled himself on Lord Byron, to Molly's delight.

Approaching middle age brought him minor ailments. Constipation was one, and piles another. Kneeling would pain his knee. Rush and bustle left him breathless, his heart pounding. He was given to flatulence after cabbage and cider. Kidney trouble too, and a stich in his side. Sciatica troubled him in the left gluteal muscle, but this was hereditary: his father too had been bothered by sciatica, measuring the changing seasons by his state of pain. Wore catskin in his waistcoat and rubbed dog spittle on the spot.

Once on wakening he had failed to recognise the room he slept in. On other occasions on waking he had been unable to move. Even from sleep-walking he was not immune, rising from bed and sitting down by a long dead fire. So, almost inevitably, he was attracted by the large claims of patent medicine and wonder drugs. He would write off for these. Protectives from Box 32, Post Office, Charing Cross. Wonderworker for rectal complaints, the world's greatest remedy, Coventry House, South Place London EC. South Place Ethical Society. He fussed over minor complaints such as a bee sting on Whit Monday, which he had examined by Dixon, the medical man he had met after the Boer War riots in 1899, now at the Mater Hospital up the road in Eccles Street.

The feeding of this frame deserved special attention from Mr Bloom. Unlike so many of his countrymen whose idea of a good meal was an overcooked beefsteak, he loved offal, as the English always call the inner organs of beasts, fowls and fishes. Kidneys (which no doctor can bring himself to eat), giblet soup, gizzards, hearts, livers, roes, blood sausages, pig's trotters, oxtails, tripes (done three ways), lights, brains and brawn. He would consider with relish the exotic fare of foreign nations, parts peculiar consumed in peculiar parts: sheeps' eyes, pigs' bladders, cows' udders, lights, white kidneys, and bulls' pistles. Many mornings while his wife breakfasted on weak tea and toast, Bloom would consume a blood-gorged kidney, eating with relish.

Other tastes could be cooled by the narcotic drift of cigar nicotine through the blood. The arty theosophical crowd around AE (Albert Edward Russell, Bloom believed) had taken up vegetarianism, whole foods for whole minds, pure nutrients for fine souls. Then there were the policemen and civil servants living on a diet of white bread and Irish stew. We are what we eat, someone once said, and Mr Bloom thought that aesthetes and policemen could be called in evidence of this. Sometimes observing with disgust the public eating habits of his fellow citizens, he would have taken to carrot crunching and greencud chewing, or garlic eating, even if he smelt like an Italian organ grinder.

Organ grinding was, in a way, a talent of Mr Bloom's. He could play upon the piano, but his own poor instrument was more adapted to solo performances than grand concerts. His home pottering and kitchen foraging suggested a Jewish streak in Bloom. His erotic habits were of a peculiar kind, involving as they did his wife's foot, boots covered in dung and other quiet horrors. A homebody was Mr Bloom. It looked as if Eccles Street would suit very well, even if they had to take in lodgers. His commission from the paper kept them going, but there was also his insurance and the Canadian bonds (bought with the money from the hotel, sold after his father died). He had accumulated these resources by thrift. His raincoat was purchased in the Lost Property Office Sale, and he would never spend money on tickets for anything if he could wangle a pass, whether for the train, the theatre or even to see Guinness' Brewery. At home too he was careful. Though they had moved a lot, their special mementoes travelled along with them. A narcissus purchased at an auction on the quays, the owl which had been a wedding present, the piano on which he sometimes accompanied Molly's singing.

There was a garden to the Eccles Street house, a large enough one with an apple tree. Bloom had plans for the garden, though as yet it only grew mint (sauce for the lamb). He planned to have a summerhouse and to grow scarlet runners and Virginia creeper. But the soil was poor and would require a great deal of work. It would need a load of dung, or lime of sulphur. Then he could have peas and lettuce as well, and greens. When optimistic he had great plans; at other times he could only see the disadvantages. Bees too might be kept.

His other plans, often unfulfilled, included a trip to see his friend Philip Shaw in Mullingar, either by foot, cycle, or barge. A trip to London — the long way round by sea — was another plan. Or if he had commission enough one day to take Molly to Margate or Brighton or Hastings.

Schemes for Mr Bloom were an easy matter. He was given to utopian elaborations, such as providing mobile toilets for ladies on the tram system. Other schemes: education, literature, journalism, prize titbits, up-to-date billing, hydros and concert tours in English watering places (Harrogate, Malvern), theatres packed with visitors, with Madame Bloom in special billing. An opening was all he wanted: ever.

Diet and self-help were the keys to Bloom's view of life. Healthy citizens and a healthy state. Though all his life had been passed in the city of Dublin — and he was now settled well within the old canal limits of that city — his ultimate ambition had, by his fortieth birthday, become the dream of a small house — Bloom Cottage, chez Leopold, Flowerville, Dunrovin, Leoville, Marion Lodge.

This home was well furnished in his dream, the garden and the house both. A two-storied thatched house was what he imagined, perhaps in Dundrum or Sutton, five minutes from the train or tram. He would have a parrot; tulips, crocuses, sweet pea, lily of the valley — bulbs and seeds from Mackeys in Sackville Street. There he could potter in his all-wool garments (such as recommended by G.B. Shaw) with elastic-sided garden boots. In the evenings he could pursue photography, comparative study of religions, folklore of sex, astronomy. Purchased by mortgage, this house might well be obtained by some windfall, the provenance of which could be any of the following:

—a scheme for radioing results to Dublin of a long-odds horse in time for bets, taking advantage of time difference between Dunsink and Greenwich Mean Time

—a rare stamp

—antique ring

—inheritance of Spanish prisoner's mysterious fortune

—a contract to deliver 32 loads at geometrically rising prices

—breaking the bank at Monte Carlo.

Other schemes included the recycling of human excrement, some 350,883,800 tons per day.

Naturally enough Molly regarded these schemes as so much nonsense, but they were an essential feature of Bloom's mental outlook. He was interested in ingenious ideas and money-making schemes and was full of scientific curiosity. Politically he was a reformer, a species of Fabian perhaps and still a supporter of Home Rule for Ireland. An extension of this was his outlook on religions (agnostic but curious) and on people (curious but astringent).

His temperament was humanely compounded of pity and sympathy, respect for others' social consciousness, family love and loyalty. He was fastidious and humourous, melancholic and sensual. But he was also imaginative, with established tastes in literature, music and art. He was interested in language and concerned with philosophical matters. But he felt keenly the lack of a serious companion with whom he could discuss these matters.

Hence an encounter in the summer of 1904 seemed to Bloom to open up new possibilities at a time of domestic strain, itself the odd result (the pattern of life again) of a meeting some months before.

... *Intermezzo: Molly and Boylan*

In September 1903 Bloom had a momentous encounter at his tailors, George S. Mesias, 5 Eden Quay (where his partner was a man named Haddock — old fishface as Simon Dedalus called him.) Bloom was having his trousers altered (at the good sum of eleven shillings). While fitting them, Mr Mesias observed that Mr Bloom was one in a million: his testicles hung on the right side.

It was while cogitating on this strange fact — one in a million — that Mr Mesias pointed out another customer.

'Boylan, Hugh Boylan. Blazes to my friends and enemies. Haven't I seen your wife sing? Madame Marion Bloom. I knew I had.'

Boylan had been present at one or two of Molly's concerts. She had talents, he hastened to explain, which were altogether admirable. Bloom was pleased, as anyone would be, at this delicate praise of his wife. He was not to know this was the beginning of an affair that would be of central importance to their lives.

Soon after this Bloom encountered Boylan once again, in the Bleeding Horse, a public house in Camden Street, near Kelly's corner. During their conversation the possibility of Boylan arranging a tour in the provinces featuring Madame Bloom was mooted. Bloom mentioned that Molly had sung in the Jesuit Church in Gardiner Street — a signal honour for her.

This had been arranged by Bloom himself through the good offices of Father Farley. The occasion was a sermon preached by Fr Bernard Vaughan, a fashionable preacher from London. His text was on Christ or Pilate — Church or State. Bloom had let it be known that he was putting 'Lead

Kindly Light' to music. In fact he concocted a tune from an old opera. Molly got to sing with the choir, but not before it had been reported to the Jesuits that Bloom was a free-mason. Father Farley was not amused and later Bloom felt that perhaps he should have approached Father Conmee about the matter. The organist that night was old Mr Glynn, who got fifty pounds a year for his trouble. Father Vaughan provided some amusement with his cockney accented version of scripture: 'Pilate! Why don't you 'old back that 'owling mob?' But he was a good and much admired man, with a kind regard for the Irish.

Then Molly sang. The 'Stabat Mater' of Rossini: *qui est homo*, the first soprano part, a magnificent performance that held the wandering attention of the church. Bloom lent his ear to the marble lined wall of the nave the better to hear the trill of her notes. Her performance added much to her laurels, before an audience crowded with *cognoscenti*. Opinion was unanimous that she was incomparable. Had they not been in church, they would have called for an encore. But Gardiner Street was not the Antient Concert Rooms.

All this Bloom related to Boylan. But Hugh Boylan's interest in Mrs Bloom was of a more direct and carnal nature. Sometime in May of 1904, in the DBC restaurant in Dame Street, the occasion came when Bloom could at last introduce Hugh Boylan to Molly. This occasion was marked by a contretemps.

Nature calling in an urgent way, Molly had to hurry off to the toilet. But there she found herself incommoded by the black closed breeches Bloom had made her buy. These took so long to let down that she wet herself. And in her discomfort she left her gloves behind. (Bloom wished to advertise for these in the *Irish Times: lost* in the ladies lavatory DBC Dame Street, finder return to Mrs Marion Bloom, 7 Eccles Street. She demurred. You never knew what mad men might take it upon themselves to write, what sort of objectionable things could arrive by every post.)

Boylan professed to be enchanted by her feet and later talked of their wonderful shape (in shoes that were too tight a fit, Molly recalled). They ordered two teas and talked again of music and concerts.

For two days Molly returned to take tea in the DBC in the hope of meeting Boylan again. This she might have done, as he worked in an advertising agency, The Advertising Co., Ltd., at 19 D'Olier Street. 'A bill sticker' his enemies called him derisively. But Mr Boylan was a man of parts, public and private.

Aside from his actual work and his musical avocation, on the side he managed a prize fighter named Myler Keogh, 'Dublin's Pet Lamb'. The month of April he had spent down in Carlow getting Myler up to scratch and fighting fit. Though Boylan forbade Keogh anything in the way of drink, he passed round the rumour that he was 'on the beer', thus running up the betting odds in his own favour.

On 22 May Keogh fought Percy Bennett, an English sergeant-major out of Portobello Barracks in Rathmines. Keogh thrashed him and Boylan won over a hundred pounds. On his winnings he grandly took the Blooms out to a fish dinner (a night Molly recalled because of the barrister they saw ambling out of Hardwicke Lane with his silk hat, and the whore trailing after him).

A week later, on the Sunday night, 29 May, Boylan and the Blooms went together to a dance. Coming back along the Tolka Boylan gave her hand a squeeze, while Molly was singing 'The Young May Moon'. She squeezed back. Bloom was aware of this carry-on: that night on their return he roused himself sufficiently to achieve, not intercourse, but to spend himself on her rear end. He was no fool: he had eyes. But it might be an opportunity for Molly: he was prepared to connive at an affair, even to the extent of sending Milly away, and absenting himself from the house until quite late on the days Boylan called 'to discuss the details of the tour' as Molly would put it. How, and where and when Boylan put it, Bloom tried not to think of.

On the night of 15/16 June, the Blooms dreamed dreams. They had been out to a concert with a strange kind of music. Bloom dreamt that he approached Molly in a turkish costume with slippers and red trousers, a jacket stitched with gold. A yellow cummerbund around her waist, a white yashmak over her face. Her feet bound by fetters: the slave of love.

And Molly dreamt a dream with (as she vainly tried to

recall) 'something about poetry'. She was to have an assignation the next day with Boylan, who also returned the next Monday. By then a new figure had appeared upon the scene: the young poet Stephen Dedalus.

The affair with Boylan took its course. A picnic in the Furry Glen, another in the Strawberry Beds, with Mrs Fleming (their part-time domestic in Eccles Street) to make up the party. On 23 June Molly and Boylan left for Belfast, not without some worry, for the first concert. There had been an outbreak of smallpox, and this might have affected their concert. But all went well.

Indeed so well that Molly contemplated eloping with Boylan, and divorcing Leopold. But even concert parties have their end. Hugh Boylan soon wearied of the voluptuous charms of Madame Bloom. She discovered him *in flagrante delicto* with another singer the following winter and promptly broke off the affair. On June 27 Bloom went as usual to Ennis for the vigil of his father's death. He visited the grave and paid the attendant for its upkeep. He too thought about leaving Molly. But after sixteen years, it would have been too great a break. Brooding on his father's fate, he returned to Dublin, having formed the complacent resolution 'to stick things out'.

1907

Waste Paper, Waste Baggings, Waste of All Descriptions. Old Books and Manuscripts, Destruction Guaranteed. Bought for Cash. M. Duan, and Co., 1 South Prince's Street.

James Hill & Son, Auctioneers, Complete House Furnishers. Est. 1810. Everybody is invited to inspect our New Furnished Model Houses, namely:—
The "Bungalow" marvellously furnished for — £59.10.0
The "Villa" most completely furnished for — £125.0.0
The "Homestead" with Period Rooms furnished for — £250. 0. 0

Old Irish Stories, Ancient Laws and Customs, including:— Lia Fail, Cuchulain, Cormac, Grace O'Malley, The Ape of Kildare, Old Laws, Irish Doctors, Fergus Roy, the Poet King, The Danes, The Druids and Their Customs, Brian Boru, Great Books of Ireland, Historical Women, Finn and His Companions, The Ancient Fairs, Children of Usnach, Bailie Mac Buain, King Daithi, etc., with Literary, Historical and Geographical Notes and Vocabulary. Crown 8vo. Illustrated. 1s. 0d.
Sullivan Brothers, Educational Publishers, 85 Abbey Street, Dublin.

Plate Glass & Window Glass of every description, also Leaded Lights, *Ecclesiastical and Domestic, manufactured on the premises. Samples and Designs free. Martins, 11 Stephen's Green, Dublin.*

Catholic Religious Articles. Important to Wholesale Purchasers.

T.D. O'Carroll, 34 Westmoreland Street, Dublin. Sole Agents in Ireland for:

Ouvry Fils Ainé, Ambert, France. *In Rosary Beads — Coco, Cocotine, Nacre. Speciality — Cocotine, and Lower Priced Rosaries.*

Fritz Iding, Kevalaer, the *Manufacturer of Crucifixes. In Crucifixes where Nickel Figures are required, buyers will find this firm the cheapest and best of all.*

Quitmann & Co., Duisberg, Germany. *This firm has a world-wide reputation as Manufacturers of Nickel and Brass* Mission Crosses. *The Wholesaler who does not know Quitmann and Co., samples is not "up-to-date".*

Künzli Frères, Zurich. *The Religious Pictures — Oleographs, Photogravures, and Aquarelles — produced by this firm have been recommended to this Catholic Country by various missioners, whose object it has been to advocate the use of Pictures that are really* DEVOTIONAL, *as well as cheap and artistic.*

H. Kissing, Menden, Germany. *As most of the Religious Medals and the Artistic Crosses sold to the public in the United Kingdom are manufactured by this Firm, wholesale buyers will be glad to send me their orders or their queries.*

D. Cullen (late F. O'Hara) window Blind Manufacturer, Repairs a speciality. Estimates Free. 23 South King Street.

8

Death

The affair between Molly and her tour manager Boylan became the talk of those circles in which the Blooms moved. But Mr Bloom's affairs were never talked of, as Mr Bloom was a discreet and careful gentleman.

In June 1904 Bloom inserted an advertisement in the *Irish Times:*

> *Wanted* smart lady typist to aid gentleman in literary work.

To this he received numerous replies including one from Lizzie Twigg, who wrote: 'My literary efforts have had the good fortune to meet with the approval of the eminent poet AE (Mr George Russell).' But this good lady seemed too earnest — she would likely be the type who would have no time to do her hair and would pass her morning over a volume of poetry. He left her unanswered.

From among forty other answers, he selected one from a Miss Martha Clifford, who lived in Dolphin's Barn, the same district in which the Tweedys had lived when Bloom had first met Molly in the summer of 1887, so long ago.

Some letters survive from the beginning of this affair. Bloom, careful as ever, wrote his letters over the pseudonym of Henry Flower, a neat transformation of his own name. Martha's third letter survives — dated 2 June 1904, care of the Post Office, Westland Row. This Mr Bloom collected on the 16th before going on to the funeral of his old friend Paddy Dignam.

Dear Henry,

I got your last letter to me and thank you very much

for it. I am sorry you did not like my last letter. Why did you enclose the stamps? I am awfully angry with you. I do wish I could punish you for that. I called you naughty boy because I do not like that other world. Please tell me what is the real meaning of that word. Are you not happy in your home you poor little naughty boy? I do wish I could do something for you. Please tell me what you think of poor me. I often think of the beautiful name you have. Dear Henry, when will we meet? I think of you so often you have no idea. I have never felt myself so much drawn to a man as you. I feel so bad about. Please write me a long letter and tell me more. Remember if you do not I will punish you. So now you know what I will do to you, you naughty boy, if you do not write. O how I long to meet you. Henry dear, do not deny my request before my patience are exhausted. Then I will tell you all. Goodbye now, naughty darling. I have such a bad headache today and write *by return* to your longing

Martha.

P.S. Do tell me what kind of perfume does your wife use. I want to know.

To this, after the funeral and his lunch, Bloom replied.

Dear Mady,

I got your letter and flower. It is utterly *impossible* to write today. You know what I mean. Accept my poor present: post office order for 2/6d. Write me a long letter. Do you despise me? I am so excited. Why do you call me naughty? You are naughty too. Bye for today. I want you to write, to keep it up. Call me that other name. You must believe, it is true. It will excite me. You know how.

In haste,
Henry.

P.S. You punish me? Tell me. I want to know. Of course, if I didn't I wouldn't ask.

H.

P.P.S. I feel so sad today. So lonely.

He wondered about her mentality. He dreamt about her at

night. She was his secret. Bloom, now at the mercy of *two* women's questions, began to live even more intently in his own secret world.

He would follow women in the streets, gaze on young girls on the beach, dream of orgies with opulent ladies in theatre boxes. Most of the time he *did* nothing about his daydreams, but Martha was different. He longed to glimpse his mysterious correspondent.

This could easily be done, for there would surely not be so many letters left in *poste restante* in Dolphin's Barn. He took himself out there one morning after he had delivered his letter, and settled himself down for surreptitious surveillance. He had asked her to collect the letter at four o'clock, and almost on time along came a dark twenty-six year old girl, dressed soberly and unexcitingly, but as he watched from his safe vantage point Mr Bloom felt that her face had a certain sensuous charm. She came out reading the letter. Mr Bloom ducked into a newsagents, purchased a copy of the *Evening Mail*, tucked it under his arm and set out at a very discreet distance. The girl made her way across the bridge in the direction of Harold's Cross. Eventually she took out a key and opened the door of a very ordinary two storied red-brick house. The door closed behind her.

When Molly departed on her concert tour towards the end of June, Bloom, feeling himself free from observation, decided he could make another move. It would, of course, be impossible to invite Martha home to Eccles Street. The neighbours, ever curious, would be sure to notice. And on her return, however unfaithful she might have been, Molly would surely be informed of Poldy's lapse from marital decorum.

Bloom had, however, a journalist friend, who was going to London for several days, hoping (as all Dublin journalists do) to ingratiate himself into the friendship of some Flect Street editor. Bloom, making some vague remark about an interest in a change of scene, was able to borrow his keys. He'd look in, don't you know, see everything was alright.

The house was in Ranelagh, one of those small cottage-type houses that climb up the slope of the old market garden from the main road. It would do very well. Now it only remained to arrange a rendezvous.

Once he had thought he might arrange to meet her in a graveyard, love among the tombstones, the cold mineral against the warm flesh. But that would be too off-putting. No, instead he would charm her. A meeting in some secluded spot, the suggestion that they call upon his friend. Arrival at friend's residence, drinks. Unlikely return of friend leads to great intimacy. Mr Bloom planned it all in lavish and imaginative detail. Her reluctant refusal, her fading resolve, her growing passion, his hands straying where they willed. Visions of Martha with variations had entertained him for a long time: now for the real thing.

He wrote to Martha proposing a rendezvous in Saint Bartholomew's, Clyde Road, Ballsbridge, which he felt would be far enough away from their own neighbourhoods for them not to be recognised, and being a Protestant Church, they would meet no one they knew.

Martha responded with alacrity, expressing hopes for their further intimacy. A naughty thing, Bloom thought. The meeting augered well.

So one afternoon in July, Mr Bloom, Leopold the Lover, made his way across the city, descending from the tram at Ballsbridge, and walked through the quiet, respectable neighbourhood to his appointment.

The church seemed empty, but then as his eyes grew used to the gloom, he saw a woman sitting alone in one corner away from the door. He approached quietly.

'Martha?' he whispered. The figure stirred.

'I beg your pardon?' The woman looked around with a startled expression on her face.

'Oh', said Bloom, 'I thought you were an acquaintance of mine.'

'Can I help you? I'm the rector's wife.'

Bloom fled.

Martha wrote to explain. She had been overcome with doubts at the last moment. Did he really mind? Could she really trust him? She was so sorry. She had failed him.

Bloom nearly despaired, but perhaps it was to have been expected. He then began to fancy that he saw her on the streets. One night in Appian Way, an ill-lit road in the vicinity of Leeson Park, a nice neighbourhood if ever there was one, Bloom nearly spoke to a shadowy female form. But before he could even say good evening, assuming her to be a 'profession-al lady' (for there were a few of them who hung around the railings of the Protestant church nearby), he realised that it was Mrs Clinch, a very proper lady indeed, the daughter of a well-known military drunk, Major Powell. She was the sister of Bloom's racing companion, Mrs Gallagher.

This nocturnal habit of wandering the streets had begun when they lived in Holles Street. Following women about was the sort of activity that might bring him to the notice of the Dublin Metropolitan Police. But he could not stop. One night in Meath Street (a rough enough quarter), he paid a girl to say rude words to him, a task very nearly beyond her. He paid her an extra florin out of pity and she kissed his hand.

He gave up these larks after an incident early in 1904. A voice from a dark doorway inquired if there was 'Any chance of your wash'? But as they talked, she revealed a close knowledge of his private life: she even knew Molly. 'A stout lady does be with you in a brown costume.' He was put off completely. He made a future appointment but then never kept it, and later had to take steps to avoid meeting the woman on Bachelor's Walk. That was the day, he re-called, that he had met Stephen Dedalus, and later that night he had seen her again in the cabman's shelter in Beres-ford Place.

Doubtless she was insane, certainly a little peculiar. But there was something a little mad about Bloom's own activi-ties. Not just with whores. There were other things, such as the obscene telephone calls he made to Miss Dunne, Boylan's secretary at the Advertising Company in D'Olier Street. Other morbid and disgusting things shamed him in retrospect.

He could comfort himself with the thought that others did these things too. He was not the only customer of the Mutoscope arcade in Capel Street, advertised as for 'Men Only', a species of 'what the butler saw' film strip palace with smutty pictures. Willy's hat and what the naughty girls did with it, all lacey lingeries and curvaceous désha-billé.

The whores were a queer kind of reality. Imagination was often better. Martha was not the first lady he had written to. There had been others on whom he had also lavished his sinful thoughts. In 1893, during the fierce cold snap, he closed the door of the carriage of a Mrs Bellingham outside Sir Thornley Stoker's house. Discovering her address, he wrote her letters describing her as 'a Venus in Furs', for he had lately been reading Sacher-Masoch, admiring her full calves and fuller bottom, and seeking to defile her marriage bed.

Also: there was the Hon Mrs Mervyn Talboys, descried at a polo match in the Park (*All Ireland* v *The Rest of Ireland*), who became the recipient of obscene photographs (purchased by post from a London address). A nude senorita having intercourse with a torero: his wife, Bloom alleged in his covering letter, in which he made suggestions of an unpleasantly gross nature.

Then there was Mrs Yelverton Barry, whom he had observed from the gods of the Theatre Royal during a performance of *La Cigale et la Fourmi*. He wrote to her describing her peerless globes. He sent her a copy of *The Girl with Three Pairs of Stays* by Paul de Kock, an author much favoured by Mr Bloom at this time. He requested her to have something more than social intercourse with him on the following Thursday at four o'clock. Her husband was a barrister on the Munster Circuit and was often away. It would be simple to arrange. Signed, James Lovebirch.

Even earlier, at the time when they had just arrived in Holles Street, Bloom managed with the help of a friendly journalist on the *Daily Express* (a paper well thought of in the Castle) to obtain entry to a garden party at the Viceregal Lodge in the Phoenix Park. He was delighted to observe the antics of the Ascendancy, while helping himself in a liberal style to whatever was on offer. Over the dessert plums his eyes encountered Mrs Miriam Dandrade, a Spanish-American divorcee who lived in the Shelbourne Hotel. Her ears immediately flamed with embarrassment, and Bloom in his confusion poured mayonnaise over his fruit, thinking it was custard; for their last meeting had been at the hotel, where Bloom had purchased from her her old wraps and black underclothes. One does not like to be reminded of such *sub rosa* activities at a viceregal garden party!

Indeed an interest in ladies' underwear was one of Mr Bloom's more partial tastes, one difficult to share. Underwear of all kinds, his wife's, on display, second-hand, glimpsed as a typist ran up the stairs, or a girl lounged on the beach. Dreams of depravity haunted him. It was a taste which he firmly believed had its origins in his friendship during the school play so long ago, with Gerard, dear Ger-Ger of the haunted eyes. Emotions recalled led to only one thing, the discharge of his feelings. To arouse himself he collected undesirable items from newspapers, magazines and purveyors of facetiae: photos of nuns, Spanish ladies, items about corporal punishment in girls' schools. Whatever Pisser Burke had once had to tell the city about Bloom was hardly even the half of it.

But the other half, so far as Bloom was concerned, was his real love for his family, and especially for his daughter Milly. Bloom's private fantasies were only a part of his life. A circumscribed sexual life was largely responsible. This had enlarged, since the onset of Milly's puberty in September 1903, to encompass a complete lack of mental intercourse between Leopold and Molly.

Milly's future concerned her parents, even as they wondered about their own. Early in 1904, her father arranged a job for her as a photographer's assistant in Mullingar, Co. Westmeath, a quiet midlands town, out of what Molly considered to be misguided family loyalty, his recollection of the long abandoned Virag photographic atelier in Hungary. Molly, who had never been taught to do anything herself, thought typing would be a better start in life for the girl. Leopold said, however, that the craft might well run in the family, like art in the blood. He had his way, because it suited Molly to have the girl out of the way as she contemplated her affair with Hugh Boylan. So Milly, instead of taking a course at Skerry's Secretarial College, went to Philip Shaw's photographic establishment in Mullingar. Bloom had met Shaw in the summer of 1901 when he had been down in Mullingar for a week or two giving his friend Simon Dedalus a hand in straightening out the voters' lists. Shaw was only too pleased to give Milly a place, and Bloom did not say too much about her character.

Milly, now almost fifteen, was becoming troublesome. She had taken to larking around the neighbourhood, riding

Harry Devan's bicycle around Nelson Street at night, and smoking cigarettes in the skating rink at Earlsfort Terrace. She needed some discipline, some training, something which the nuns up the road had failed to give her.

Shaw was paying her 12/6 a week, which might well have been bettered in Dublin, but she was less likely to come to harm down in the country. Or so Bloom thought. He had reckoned without the nature of young women. For her birthday on 15 June 1904, they had sent her some small presents, which she had thanked them for in her fine, careless way, in brief note.

Dearest Papli,

Thanks ever so much for the lovely birthday present. It suits me splendid. Everyone says I'm quite the belle in my new tam. I got mummy's lovely box of creams and am writing. They are lovely. I am getting on swimming in the photo business now. Mr Coghlan took one of me and Mrs will send when developed. We did great biz yesterday. Fair day and all the beef to the heels were in. We are going to lough Owel on Monday with a few friends to make a scrap picnic. Give my love to mummy and to yourself a big kiss and thanks. I hear them at the piano downstairs. There is to be a concert in the Greville Arms on Saturday. There is a young student comes here some evenings named Bannon his cousins or something are big swells he sings Boylan's (I was on the pop of writing Blazes Boylan's) song about those seaside girls. Tell him silly Milly sends my best respects. Must now close with fondest love.

Your fond daughter,
MILLY

P.S. Excuse bad writing, am in a hurry. Byby. M.

How ironic, Bloom reflected. They had sent her to the country, out of harm's way, they supposed, only for her to become involved with a student, doubtless a medical too, the worst kind, the ones who know it all. No secrets of the flesh for them!

However, as she said herself, she was 'getting on swimming in the photo business'. Indeed the shop was quite busy, especially on fair days, when the farmers would come into town from the county. Some were wealthy enough to enjoy the records provided by photographs, evidence of their position in the world. But also those who were so poor or enterprising that they had to emigrate would have a photograph taken to remind the mothers left behind of their departed features.

Phil Shaw's shop, in which was also established the Post Office, was a busy place, as he also ran a general stationary business. The stock included rosary beads, prayer books, statues, scapulars, religious pictures, and books. Mortuary habits were also retailed at 5/-, 7/1d, and 10/6d. During the summer it was his custom to travel round the county taking photographs of places for postcards and undertaking private commissions. He employed a Mr Coghlan to help him in the dark room, and Milly's job was generally to serve in the shop and to assist in the business of the darkroom.

The nature of the business brought a varied clientele into the shop. Apart from small farmers, officers from the garrison and members of the county gentry also patronised the photographer. These Milly would have to deal with, taking down the details in the order book and fixing appointments for the sessions. These days, as her father had explained to her, photography was not a matter of a forty minutes pose as it had been in his cousin's atelier in Hungary. Now nearly instantaneous, the fixed image of the features could be available in a few minutes. When she arrived and Shaw was explaining the work to her, he took a photograph of Milly, which she was able to send to her parents in Dublin.

For a young girl Mullingar might well have seemed a very dull place indeed. But Milly soon found that aside from Mr Shaw's own family, there were lively young people of her own age around her.

Among those who came in in the evening was a student named Alec Bannon. His people were from the neighbourhood, but he was studying medicine in Dublin. He played the piano with considerable panache and sung a song which she had heard from Blazes Boylan, 'Those lovely seaside girls'. It always made her smile, reminding her of outings to Bray in the summer. On Saturday evenings there would be a concert, sometimes in the Greville Arms. The July of 1904 was made memorable for Milly by a scrap picnic at

Lough Owel, with the Shaw girls and some others, including Alec Bannon.

She wore the new tartan Tam O'Shanter which she had been sent for her birthday. She wore her navy skirt which came to her calf and, as it was a hot day, her thin white blouse, opened at the neck to show her bosom. A girl had to look attractive after all. They went out to the lake by trap. The rugs were spread and the picnic laid out. The men had brought their bathing things and retired conveniently behind some bushes to change their apparel. How well Bannon looked, Milly had thought, an athletic, well-built man. He talked of joining the army, buying a commission and going abroad. Milly fondly imagined him in uniform. He looked well in his tweed shorts and brogues, not to speak of his striped woollen bathing suit which clung dramatically to the body when wet. But in a uniform!

And afterwards, they slipped away (not unnoticed, of course) to walk through the woods, where mushrooms or berries might be found, or wild strawberries. They sat down to admire the light glinting on the lake, Alec spreading out his jacket to save her skirt. He took her hand, and said how smart she looked, her fair hair, her pretty scarf. He kissed her cheek lightly, then seeing she did not resist, kissed her on the mouth. She counted his kisses — this was the third. She lay back on the coat, her blouse loose at her throat, her breasts standing up through the thin fabric. He would not have been a man if he had not touched, his finger moving over those finely shaped features, the wild red strawberries. But no, he could not put his hand inside, not this time.

A summer romance with a little cuddling and harmless fondling — this was all very well. But soon other events would recall Milly from the shop at Mullingar. She came back to Dublin, obtained a better position in Chancellor's and later still moved on to Lawrence's. By then she herself was able to take many of the routine photographs in which little artistry was required, such as for students from the universities, who were content to pose before a half-drop and a papier-mâché pillar.

Alec Bannon went abroad as he had planned. He had written a few times, but by then she was casting her glances elsewhere. A careful child, however: no man ever got too close to her, even on long country ambles or walks in the Phoenix Park. A little fun was all very well, but a girl had to think of her future, and what a husband might feel. And then her parents might disapprove, especially her mother.

Molly, meanwhile, untroubled since the death of Rudy by the sexual attentions of her husband (except for the occasional unsuccessful effort), sought her satisfaction elsewhere. Aside from her affair with Gardner, she had been loyal to Leopold until the advent of Blazes Boylan. What he had that Leopold lacked was clear enough to anyone who saw him sauntering round the streets of Dublin that summer.

With Boylan she had planned out the concert tour which was to mark her return to the stage. It would be a tour of the chief provincial towns, arranged by Louis Verner, with such top rank artists as J.C. Doyle and John McCormack, from the end of June 1904 on, with part shares and part profits arranged by Blazes Boylan. She had by then not sung for over a year (not since an appearance at St Teresa's Hall in Clarendon Street).

The tour, duly organised, set out on its round of Irish cities and towns, the enchanting figure of Madame Bloom making a great impression wherever they went. The tour proved to be a success, profitable for all concerned.

These concert parties became an annual event with Madame Bloom for four years, although the toll on her health was greater than anyone had imagined. She had first begun to worry about her health at the end of 1903. Her periods had become irregular, and she began to fret, as so many women do, that she had some morbid condition in her insides. She went to the doctor, who calmly reassured her on this point, and took her two guineas. But the unaccustomed travelling and the bad food that was endemic in Irish hotels was not what he might have ordered for her complete recovery.

At this time too there was the strain of her scheme to turn the house in Eccles Street into either apartments or lodgings. They attempted to rent the apartments, but there was very little interest taken in them until the summer of 1904. On one of his excursions at night, Leopold had made the acquaintance of the young poet Stephen Dedalus, the son of his old friend Simon Dedalus. Stephen was in an unsettled frame of mind, brought on by the death of his mother some time before. Bloom brought him back for cocoa, and subsequently he offered Stephen the use of one of their rooms at a much reduced rent (which, even so, often went unpaid). So Mr Dedalus came to stay, much to the intrigued interest of Madame Bloom.

The poet installed himself and his manuscripts in one of the upstairs rooms and settled down, so he claimed, to a period of intensive work. Among the products of his effort were some stories which he published in the *Irish Homestead,* a series of four in all, which Mr Bloom read with great interest. The young man clearly had talent. Mrs Bloom wondered if he would ever see in her a figure of literature, the great love of a young man's life. What wouldn't Paul de Kock have made of such a situation? What could she make of it herself?

For Stephen, Molly represented a somewhat dubious figure. She would wander round the house in a state of contrived negligence, carefully preening herself to impress him. Stephen, however, had other interests. His writing took up his time, and then later in the summer he began to see a great deal of a young woman. At her age, Molly had few attractions beside a girl of eighteen. In September he left the house in Eccles Street. Shortly after, the Blooms heard that he had left Ireland for the continent with the girl. Leopold was told in passing that Simon Dedalus had reported that the girl was a nobody, some country creature who had been a chambermaid in the City Arms Hotel.

Molly's brief affair with Boylan in the summer of 1904 had broken the last major emotional bond that tied her to her husband. For the next few years, the Blooms' life settled into the complacent rhythm of a loveless marriage. They tolerated one another and stayed together, partly in deference to social convention, partly out of the residual sense of security they drew from one another.

Molly continued to worry about her health. Her periods never became regular again and she suffered occasional bouts of mysterious pain, which seemed to her to increase in frequency as the years passed. She had no faith in doctors, least of all after the cool way the last one had relieved her of two guineas and told her she was all right when she knew herself that *something* was the matter. But whatever it was, it did not normally distress her enough to disrupt her routine, although from 1907 on she found that she could only keep up the house and suit the tenants by taking on a maid. Eventually, early in 1909, Leopold prevailed on her to see a doctor once more, in the hope that the trouble could be identified and cured.

Tests were made and analysed and once again, she was assured that everything was in order, but this time, unknown to her, the doctor sent for Leopold a few days after the consultation.

'I am afraid', he said gravely, 'that the news of your wife is not quite as good as I told her.'

Bloom paled. 'What's wrong with her?'

The doctor said calmly, 'I have to tell you that she has cancer. It has obviously been. . .'

'Oh God', said Bloom weakly.

The doctor continued. 'It has obviously been developing for some time. It's always worse in a young person, grows with them and can be terribly hard to identify.'

'Has she any chance at all?' said Bloom, quietly, gaping past the doctor's shoulder and out the window.

'I must be frank, Mr Bloom. Your wife will not survive this illness. My guess is that she has about a year, perhaps eighteen months, two years if she is very lucky. She won't feel too bad for another few months but thereafter she will weaken progressively.'

Bloom stared past him at the garden, stirring itself in early spring. He said nothing.

'I am very sorry' said the doctor.

'Why did you not tell her yourself?' asked Bloom.

'I think she knows instinctively anyway, but to tell her now would be to burden her few remaining months of normal life with the certain knowledge of. . .' He fidgeted with his waistcoat buttons and his voice trailed off.

Bloom left, resolved not to tell Molly, confused, upset, lonely. He thought of stopping for a drink on his way home, then changed his mind. Bad idea to reach for a bottle in a crisis.

What would he do? Try to live normally for as long as possible and then. . . . Molly and he would be twenty-one years married the coming autumn. Their lives had drifted apart in many ways, but still, twenty-one years. . . . He could no longer imagine ordinary life without her.

Their anniversary came and went and still Molly kept going, increasingly showing the strain of her illness. The last flash of energy came in January 1910 when she read in the *Freeman's Journal* of a new public entertainment available to Dubliners. It was a cinema, the city's first, which had been opened in Mary Street by a group of Austrian entrepreneurs. Leopold was less than impressed. 'They must have great courage or great cash to come all this way to open such a thing. In Mary Street too. There aren't many people who would want to wander down there late at night. They have been ill advised to open in such a quarter. Why not Mabbot Street while they are about it.'

'Oh, Poldy let's go. It sounds so exciting.'

It was called the Volta Electric Theatre. A small string orchestra was playing a waltz as they came in. The house was painted tastefully in crimson and light blue. They chose the best seats at sixpence (rather than those on the benches at fourpence and tuppence). They noted that the programmes were available from 5 pm, every hour, and that the films were changed weekly, as was the continental system. By the time they got there, the initial programme which had been reviewed in the paper had been changed; a film about orphans and *The Tragic Story of Beatrice Cenci* had given way to *Nero* and a film about the Italian navy.

Molly was thrilled: 'Oh Poldy, are they real?' she whispered, astonished at the liveliness of the moving pictures. Coming away they noticed that *Fatal Forgetfulness* and *The Abduction of Miss Berrelli* were promised for the future. The films seemed strange and suggested whole areas of experience which could hardly be conceived. They were not merely a novelty, for Bloom realised that in that darkened hall a modern world was being created which had little to do with their easy old ways. The quickened pulse of modern times had begun to beat in the body of Irish life. What would another century make of a film record of Dublin life in

108

1910, he wondered. It was, Bloom thought, a good business to be in. Other cinemas came and went, but during Bloom's life the Volta — the only original — remained (closing only in 1948).

That was the last time Leopold and Molly Bloom went out in public together. By the end of January, she had weakened visibly, and she was confined to bed from early February. As the doctor had predicted, she knew she was dying.

'I'm not going to get better, Poldy, am I?' she said.

'No, Molly dear, I'm afraid not.'

Molly did not linger. By the second week of April her mind had begun to wander and on the 24th she died. Her last words were 'Oh Poldy, the sailors were so nice.' She was within six months of her fortieth birthday.

1912

The House for Modern Art Needlework, Materials and Requisites for Irish Laces. Moneypenny's, 39 Grafton Street, 39, Dublin. Terms Cash. No Accounts.

Shamrock Motor and Cycle Works, Marks Lane, Great Brunswick Street, Dublin. Makers of the Famous Shamrock Cycles. Prices £10. 10s. 0d. and £12. 12s. 0d.

Crosse & Blackwell's. Purveyors to His Majesty the King. C & B Pickles. Morrison's Quay, Cork.

Thomas Heiton & Co., Ltd. Heiton's House Coals are the very best on the market. Special attention paid to loading coals in Railway Wagons. Double Screened for Country. Over screens specially built at our Spencer Dock Wharf to ensure coal being loaded is entirely free from slack.

Lambert, Brien & Co., Ltd. Camphor Soap Candles. Manufacturers of the famous Ballroom Polish which produces a Perfect Dancing Floor by simply Sprinkling. 64 Grafton Street, Dublin.

Damp Buildings Made Damp Proof By Using Hunters's Damp Resisting Rubber Silicate and Stone Preservative. Irish Manufacture. Telephone 3239. Est. 1855. William Hunter & Sons, 63 & 64 Mabbot St., Dublin.

Rudall, Carte & Co., Ltd. Band Instruments and Bagpipes. Made and Repaired on the Premises. 7 Queen Street, Dublin.

The same position as last year, but with more new ideas to increase your Business. If you want Real Good Photos. Well Sir! Roe MacMahon, 11 Harcourt Street. He can do them Properly.

National Association for the Employment of Reserve and Discharged Soldiers. 23 Great Brunswick Street, Dublin. There are at present many deserving ex-soldiers registered on the books of this association, who are desirous of employment in the following capacities:—

    Porters, Messengers, Caretakers, Nightwatchmen, Grooms, Clerks, Rural Postmen, Van drivers, etc.

If employers of labour at any time require men to fill such situations they should apply to the Hon. Secretary, 23 Great Brunswick Street. No fees are charged, and only men of bona fide good character recommended.

    Employers should note that Soldiers have every opportunity for improving themselves educationally during their service with the Colours, and receive instruction in their respective trades they are likely to follow in after life.

    For the above reasons employers of labour should recommend respectable and intelligent young men to become soldiers, so as to save themselves the trouble and expense of tuition.

Lalouette & Co. North Prince's Street (Near G.P.O.) Livery and Carriage establishment. Convenient to all Theatres and for Dances, etc. Motors stored. Nightman. Est. 121 years.

9

Rudy Redux

The death of Madame Bloom, the noted concert singer, was naturally reported in the *Freeman's Journal*, and the funeral was a crowded one. Faces from the past, almost forgotten in the passage of time, offered their condolences. Josie Powell (Mrs Breen as she was now), John Henry Menton, Atty Dillon. . . . But for Leopold and Milly the aftermath was difficult. The house in Eccles Street was given up. It was too large for them to manage, and, in any case, Milly was now contemplating marriage. An end merged into a beginning.

Through her job she had become involved with a cycling club. In that decade before the War, the bicycle was all the rage, providing a cheap means of mobility and freedom to wander the countryside, with copies of *Ann Veronica* tucked into capacious pockets. Saturday companions could become passionate friends. While on a cycling excursion to Glendalough, Milly made the acquaintance of a young civil servant. She had begun to go about with him in a decorous manner (the New Woman was all very well, but Dublin was Dublin after all). She soon brought him home to meet her parents.

Jeremiah Florence McCarthy was (inevitably) from Cork, a city remote from the experience of the Blooms. He was a young man of vigorous opinions, one of the New Men. The first time he called he had expressed himself quite forcefully over the tea things about the problem in Limerick. The 'problem in Limerick' had been a Jewish one.

In January 1904, a passion-struck Redemptorist priest had preached a sermon accusing the Jews of wicked business practices, the shedding of Christian blood, and warning that they would kidnap and slay Christian children. The Redemptorists had been expelled from France by Republicans —

some of whom were Jews — and the good Fr Creagh hoped to attack them by attacking those Jews nearer to hand. A boycott was organised in the city against the Jewish shops. A gang of louts stoned the Rabbi, Elias Ben Levin, and two of his friends. There were thirty Jewish families in the city. The boycott lasted two long years, driving out eighty members of a community which numbered less than 120. Shops were closed, families reduced to poverty.

Milly's young man was inclined to follow the line in Arthur Griffith's paper, the *United Irishman*, that Jews were part of a system of international userers from which the Irish peasant ought to be relieved. Bloom, who was friendly with Griffith — a coming man he had always said to Molly — was outraged. He spluttered out a defence of his father's race. And later told Milly that she should give up the anti-semite. She would betray her blood, the blood of his ancestors, by marrying him.

But Milly was as stubborn as her mother. Parental disapproval only gave the young man a greater interest in her eyes. In any case, given a long engagement, she would not be marrying him until she was over twenty-one. He had to save first for the wedding, like a careful Corkman. There was nothing that Bloom could do, but he could never bring himself wholly to like this enthusiast for Irish freedom, whose ideas often seemed to preclude the freedom of others.

Molly died in April 1910, and after a year's mourning, Milly and her Corkman were married two weeks before her twenty-second birthday on 1 June 1911. She and her husband went to the Isle of Man for their honeymoon, and on their return set up home in Wellpark Avenue, a small red-brick terrace out in Drumcondra. This was a neighbourhood of civil servants and provincial *arrivistes*, and suited Jerry McCarthy very well. It was not, however, a house in which Mr Bloom felt he could make himself at home. Giving up the house in Eccles Street, he moved across Dorset Street to take lodgings with Mrs Mooney in Hardwicke Street. He remained in a familiar neighbourhood and pursued his old interests.

Old Mrs Mooney ran the house with a firm hand. Her daughter was married to a Mr Doran, who worked in Power's, and they had a nice little house in Phibsborough. Mrs Mooney was fond of explaining to people how lucky she was to have her daughter off her hands.

The house had a regular lot of lodgers, clerks and civil servants for the most part, though Mrs Mooney also took in travellers from England and music hall artistes. The tourists were often a bore, but the artistes lent an air of convivial vulgarity to the weekends. For of course with no theatres open on Sunday nights, they were prepared to stay in and entertain the other lodgers.

Their anecdotes of the halls enthralled Bloom. He had long hoped to do something for Michael Gunn at the Gaiety, and from what they had to say a good song for a popular artiste and a man's fortune could be made. The Royal or the Empire Palace were all very well, but heights such as the Alhambra were open to a man of talent. He would write his song for Sinbad and the other themes long left aside, and send them to Dan Leno. He would be famous. But when Monday morning would come Mr Bloom would be off to work as per usual, the songs unwritten.

The rest of the regular lodgers were a steady lot, except for Bantam Lyons. For as long as Bloom had known him (and who did not know him in Dublin, he was so constantly around the pubs and newspaper offices), Bantam Lyons had been pursuing the elusive coup of backing a winner at astronomical odds. He was always after a sure thing, always failing to bring it off. Ten years before, when they had all been that much younger, this had seemed amusing. But now in middle age, he was taking on an air of desperation.

'Not to worry, Bloom, the nag with my name on will come in one day. Our fortunes will be made.'

Bloom related to Lyons his own scheme for a betting coup. By use of wireless (Signor Marconi's useful invention would be a great improvement on the electric telegraph) they could take advantage of the time difference between London and Dublin, receiving the results of a race minutes before the time of the 'start' by Irish time. He and Lyons discussed the scheme at great length, too great length, for the plan was finally foiled when the Time (Ireland) Act came into force on 1 October 1916, extending Greenwich or Western European Time over the whole of Ireland.

The year Milly married, 1911, was enlivened for Dubliners

by a visit from the new king and queen, George and Mary. They came over to open the new College of Science, and they drove into Dublin amid scenes of great enthusiasm. They visited Trinity College, the Phoenix Park races and the Iveagh Play Centre in Francis Street. After a service in St Patrick's on Sunday they went out to Maynooth, and on to the old soldiers in the Royal Hospital at Kilmainham. One of their last acts, after other state functions, was to open the D.F. Collier Memorial Dispensary in Great Charles Street.

'And no other place ever needed one more,' said McCoy to Bloom as they discussed the royal progress one evening.

'A nice contrast between the royal pomp and Dublin's circumstance,' Bloom agreed, grinning smugly at his clever formulation.

But the Dubliners who waved their Union Jacks and shouted 'God Save the King', and even those who laughed at the polite progress of the royal couple, were not to know that this was an historic occasion, the last royal visit of an English king to Dublin city.

Bloom felt the weight of middle age descending. Already memorials to events in his youth were appearing in the city. On 1 October 1911 the statue of Charles Stewart Parnell, which was to grace the long erected pillar before the Rotunda, was unveiled by John Redmond, Parnell's successor as leader of the Irish Party.

Parnell had become by now a part of the buried past. To those of Bloom's generation, who had grown up with him at the height of his powers, who had lived through the excitement of the Land War and of his fall from grace, it was all too difficult to believe. Were they too becoming a part of the past? Still, John Redmond's leadership offered the promise of Home Rule for Ireland in the not too distant future. What that future really offered only a prophet or a planchette could tell.

Bloom, having lived through the agonies of his wife's death, had begun to take an interest in the occult. The presence of Sir William Barrett in Dublin with the Dublin Section of the Society for Psychical Research, made the subject one of considerable local interest. There had been great excitement about the poltergeist down in Enniscorthy the year before.

Mr Bloom's interest, however, was not in such demons, but in the departed dead. In his mind revenants of the dead, of his father, his son Rudy and his wife Molly, still walked. He threw himself into the bizarre anecdotes of death and return recorded in Frederick Myers' large work on *Human Personality and Its Survival of Bodily Death* in the National Library. Inevitably he fell in with a group who held regular seances in a house out in Rathgar.

On his first visit to this group Bloom was disappointed. The spirits were restless and uncommunicative. The planchette was attempted, but from the disordered letters they could spell out nothing that made sense.

'It is not quite what I expected, Mrs Hume,' Bloom remarked to the medium over tea afterwards.

'We cannot expect to break across the barrier of matter so easily as you imagine, Mr Bloom. We must be patient and in time all will be revealed. The spirits must test us. They do not care to deal with the merely frivolous. But no one of us here would approach communion with the Great Beyond in such a flippant manner.'

On the next occasion the spirits spoke. But it was not Molly, or anyone he knew, but the dead daughter of Mrs Maguire. The high, squeaky voice spoke of death, great death, of terrible turmoil, of great lights, turmoil and a new order. It was a quite frightening experience, for all his doubts, especially as the portents in the daily papers were almost as bad.

Bloom began to see in every new event a confirmation of what the voice had said. The sinking of RMS *Titanic* on the night of 15 April 1912, with the loss of over 1,500 people — many of them impoverished emigrants from Ireland, where the ship had been built, was the greatest disaster of its kind in human history. It was an appalling shock.

'What can we expect next?' mused Bloom to Bantam Lyons. This ship had been the epitome of modern achievement and social order, but it had been wrecked on an iceberg by the unexpected and by human error. Other icebergs might lie in wait for them all.

'No, no, Bloom, it was a judgment,' Lyons claimed. 'Did you not know that she was launched in Belfast with "No Pope" written up on her side. No ship could be lucky with such a start!'

117

'Was that a fact?' said Bloom. Was that a fact? Knowing Lyons, some small glint of reality had possibly been wildly distorted. But one could believe anything of them up in Belfast, where the rise of the extreme Protestant Orange Order was looked upon with dismay from Dublin.

The wild claims of the Orangemen seemed to belong, with Parnell, to some past life. On 26 April the first aeroplane flew across the Irish Sea between Holyhead and Dublin in an hour and a quarter. Man had triumphed once again over nature. Perhaps, mused Bloom, with the same application, the same resolution in the face of defeat, he could solve such merely political problems as loomed up out of the future like icebergs.

During August 1913 Mr Bloom took his annual holiday — two weeks off for the Horse Show and the week after. On the evening of the 29th he was returning by tram from Rathgar where he had been to another table-turning session. When the tram reached Kevin Street, he noticed that the street seemed strangely crowded. Then through the window of the tram came half a brick, scattering glass around the interior. A mother with a small baby perched on her lap screamed.

'It's those bloody Larkinites,' said one of the other passengers.

'Merciful God, will they kill us all?' screamed the mother, clutching the infant to her breast.

Three days before, members of the Irish Transport and General Workers Union had gone on strike against William Martin Murphy's Dublin Tramway Company in a struggle for recognition of the union. But the trams continued to run, driven by a mixture of non-union labour and strikebreakers. The leader of the union, Jim Larkin, had made a number of impassioned speeches attacking both Murphy and the strikebreakers. Feelings were running very high.

His face bleeding from the glass, Mr Bloom tumbled out of the tram into the roadway. Escaping from the shouting and jeering mob, he made his way up along Bride Street to the Meath Hospital. In casualty, who should appear to help him but Dr Dixon.

'What have you been doing to yourself?' he asked.

'The tram I was on ran into a bit of trouble. The windows were smashed in. Glass everywhere.'

'A bad business, all this labour trouble,' the doctor remarked. 'I seemed destined to see you only when you are involved in a riot.'

'Or stung by a bee,' corrected Bloom.

'Ah, yes, there was that of course. Now this too will sting.'

But the tram strike and then the subsequent lock-out in other industries that divided Dublin for the rest of 1913 was no joking matter. After this incident, Bloom was careful to keep well away from Sackville Street or from anywhere near Beresford Place, where Jim Larkin had his trade union headquarters. He had seen enough of the violence.

In his digs, the residents returned each day with some new tale to supplement what was in the daily papers. All summer the city had been seething with labour unrest as Larkin attempted to organise the lowest paid workers in the city and on the docks. He was a man about whom there were bitterly-divided opinions. On the streets he was acclaimed a hero; in Bloom's digs, the young men whose jobs were secure enough could afford to hate him.

'William Martin Murphy is right. The man is a danger to society,' said Reynolds one evening, when he had finished reading the leader in the *Irish Independent*. 'He is an anarchist who will stop at nothing to destroy industry, home and church.'

'Did you hear the latest lark that his supporters are getting up to,' added Maguire, who was a clerk in Guinness's. 'They are taking the children of the poor away from their families and transporting them to England for a fortnight's holiday, no less. And of course, they'll all end up in Protestant houses. Bloody heathens!'

Bloom held his tongue. He recognised the hardening extremes of argument which could see no good at all in the other side's case. To Larkin, William Martin Murphy was represented as all that was foul and grasping in modern capitalism. Useless to argue that Mr Murphy, though a hard boss, had through his enterprises provided good secure jobs for nearly two generations of Dubliners. As for the pro-Murphy partisans, they blithely shut their eyes to the grind-

119

ing, desperate poverty of the slums, from which Larkin drew so many of his members.

On 2 September, as if in some diabolical comment on the poverty and squalor of parts of Dublin, a tenement house in Church Street collapsed. Seven people were killed and six injured. The municipal authorities were forced to face up to the degradation of the lost souls forced to live in the teeming slums. They did what authorities everywhere do when hard pressed: they appointed a committee to report.

But this disaster, which only illustrated the state of the city, was eclipsed by the riots of the days previous. On 31 August and 1 September, and again on 21 September, there were riots in the city centre in which 550 people, fifty of them policemen, were injured. Two of the injured later died. The police had the better of these encounters, and were denounced for their barbarity by the city council. The port of Dublin was closed from 12 October to 10 December. These struggles, followed eagerly by Bloom and his fellows in Hardwicke Street, went on until the beginning of 1914, when Larkin was forced to concede. The settlement came on 19 January.

'We should be happy that is all over,' said Bloom to the others, while reading of the settlement over breakfast in his *Freeman's Journal.*

'We should, but we won't,' said Reynolds, chasing the last bit of bacon round his plate. 'There is worse to come. Look at Ulster, armed men everywhere. And little better here, with the Volunteers and the Citizen Army and the rest of them. Mark my words, Bloom, no good will come of all these little armies.'

Bloom was depressed. There were only some 300,000 people in the city and nearly 25,000 had been thrown out of work. Everyone was affected. A sense of terror and foreboding seized many, a feeling that this display of hate and violence boded ill for the future. Perhaps Reynolds was right. This, after all, had only been a labour dispute, about which there were divided opinions. What would happen if a major passion, such as religion or nationalism, erupted on the same streets?

Could this, Bloom wondered, have been the cryptic vision given them by the spirits?

That summer the Corporation tried to redeem the reputation of the city. A Civic Exhibition was opened at the Linen Hall Barracks on 15 July. When it closed on 31 August, it had been attended by over 110,000 people. But by then the Dublin riots, which had seemed the worst of calamities, had been eclipsed by far worse events.

The Great War broke out with fearful suddeness at the beginning of August. The Horse Show was abandoned, and even the Home Rule Act, which received the royal assent on 18 September 1914, fulfilling hopes held since the days of Parnell, was put in suspense until the end of hostilities. Things must have been bad if both horses *and* politics had to take a back seat in Ireland.

For Bloom and his family the war brought further trials. Jerry McCarthy, like so many other Irishmen, felt he must answer the call to arms, to defend, not the British Empire, but the freedom of Ireland. This war against Germany was presented as a war for Christian civilisation. Some half-a-million Irishmen were under arms in the Great War, one-fifth of the total population of the island. When, at a later date, people began to talk about the Irish nation in arms, meaning some handful of fanatics with German rifles in their hands, Mr Bloom would reflect on what the nation in arms had really been.

Jerry enlisted in September 1914, and in November he was sent to the Western Front. At that time, they still talked of the 'whole show being over by Christmas'. But it was soon clear that this was not going to be the case. The armies dug in, and shelled each other hour by hour. The real hell was soon to begin.

In February 1914, Milly had given birth to a daughter, Marion, and was by Christmas six months pregnant with a second child. To help her and keep her company, Bloom moved into the house in Drumcondra while Jerry was at the front. Then in January 1915 came the news that Jerry had sustained a stomach wound, not fatal, but bad enough to bring him home for good. He was declared unfit for future service. The shock did not do Milly much good, however, and in March she was delivered of a stillborn child.

The death of this child and the trauma of Jerry's illness brought Bloom closer to the young couple. He stayed on

121

in the house, helping as best he could. He was still there in 1916 when another disaster overtook them.

Jerry's experiences in France had caused him to revise some opinions. Always a strong nationalist, he had been hardened by what he saw at the front; he came to believe that Home Rule was no longer enough and that only violence would gain Ireland real freedom. This opinion was, in a way, an Irish reflection of the policies being pursued by the imperial governments in the Great War. If violence was the way for the great powers, violence would be the way for Ireland. Jerry now supported the anti-War Irish Volunteers, but was wholly unaware of the tiny, militant minority within the Volunteers who planned a rising at Easter. Due to some last minute hitches, the rising in fact did not begin until Easter Monday, when it came like a bolt from the blue.

It was a holiday, a day on which thousands of Dubliners departed for the races at Fairyhouse and returned to find a revolution had broken out. The first that Bloom heard about it was when he strolled down to the shops to buy some small items, and found the street buzzing with rumours. There was trouble in the city centre. No it was not the trade unionists again. Some said there had been a German invasion. Then slowly the real news came through. Some Sinn Fein people had declared a Republic! The Fenians were out again!

Jerry, still recovering from his wound, was of little use to the revolutionaries. He could contact no one he knew. Communications seemed to have broken down. That week passed with rumours and counter rumours. For those not involved, the week meant no supplies, no bread, no fresh meat, hardly any milk. Jerry remarked that it was just like the war in Europe. On 29 April a fire started in Lower Sackville Street and raged through Middle Abbey Street, Sackville Place, Earl Street, Henry Street, Moore Street and Prince's Street. The British were said to have done this by shelling the rebel headquarters in the GPO.

The next day the rebels surrendered and were marched away to prison to the jeers and taunts of Dubliners who had been badly shaken by the insurrection. When the streets were open again, Mr Bloom joined the crowds surveying the damage to the city centre. Near the Rotunda he met

Simon Dedalus and they walked as far as they could along the half-ruined length of Sackville Street.

'Did you ever think we would live to see the like of this,' Bloom said. 'What was it all for?'

'I hear,' said the ever well-informed Simon, 'that the cost of it all rises towards 3 million pounds. Three million pounds! You could build a country for money like that.'

It was all so inexplicable. The damage staggered Mr Bloom; familiar haunts had been swept away in the course of a night. This, he thought, is not revolution, this is vengeance. He had just turned fifty and had become set in his widower's ways; now looking at those smouldering ruins, he saw the familiar city of his youth blasted out of existence. A little part of Bloom's generation died in 1916.

Then came the executions of the leaders. On and on they went, day after day, cruel and useless. Poor Willy Pearse, murdered because he was his brother's brother. And James Connolly, shot in a chair because his wounds would not let him stand. In relation to what was happening every day on the front, sixteen deaths seemed nothing to the stupid military mind. But they shocked Dublin, they shocked Ireland, and many who had felt grave doubts about the rising now hardened their hearts against Englishmen who had shot Irishmen in such callous circumstances.

Slowly things came back to normal, in so far as war is normal. The news from the Western Front and elsewhere during 1916 and 1917 grew worse and worse.

'What sort of madness is all of this, Jerry?' Bloom wondered. 'The generals are throwing away a generation to capture a few hundred yards of soil.'

'You do not understand the military mind. The generals are concerned with strategy, not with casualties.'

Then came the revolution in Russia, an even more terrible affair to some. The long toll of deaths, and of Irish deaths in particular, extended on into 1918. Then in October, the Germans sunk the *Leinster* while it was on its way from Kingstown to Holyhead. Some 801 people were killed that night. This was a last shock before the war came to an end on 11 November with an armistice.

For some the end of the war was marked by the election, in which Sinn Fein triumphed; for others by the celebrations of the general holiday on 19 July 1919 on the signing of the actual peace with Germany; for others, more local in their enthusiasms, the opening of the Metal Bridge on 25 March made a memorable Dublin day.

But the end of the war was marked in 1918 for Leopold Bloom by the birth of a grandson, whom they called Rudolph Florence McCarthy. Now he could hold in his arms his lost son: the Rudy who had died had been reborn. He could almost believe in metempsychosis.

1919

Dun Emer Guild Ltd., Hardwicke Street, Dublin. Handwoven Carpets, Rugs and Tapestries, Embroideries. Church banners, Colours, Flags. Costume Designers and Enamellers. The Carpets and Rugs are Hand-Made of Best Wool. Church Carpets a Speciality. Designs and Estimates Free.

Cement. War Office Restrictions removed. Permits no longer necessary. We hold good stocks of Portland Cement. Immediate delivery. Brooks Thomas & Co., Ltd, Dublin.

War Prices Will Only be Charged when Raw Materials Costing More than their Normal Price Have to be Used. Shackell, Edwards & Co., Ltd, Makers of Fine Printing Inks Since 1786.

Surgical and Rubber Appliances. Our 1918 illustrated 76 page Catalogue of Sprays, Douches, Enemas and Surgical Rubber Goods of every description sent free with Manual of Wisdom *upon application. Le Brasseur Surgical Co., Ltd. (Dept. V.D.), 90 and 92 Worcester Street, Birmingham.*

Princess, Rathmines. "Her Temptation", Fox Film featuring Gladys Brockwell. First time in Dublin. Don't Miss it. Keystone and Pathe Comedies, Gazette, Serial and Prof. Renaud's Famous Orchestra. Thurs. Mary Pickford in "M'Liss".

Roberts' Victory Sale. Now On. Grafton Street, Dublin.

Mary Street Picture House. Last Three days. Charlie Chaplin in "Shoulder Arms".

Before selecting your Household or Office Stationary, ask to see samples of the Imperial Parchment Note. The Most Popular Writing Paper of the times. Cream or Azure. Writing Pads, Correspondence Cards and Compendiums. Alex. Thom & Co., Ltd., Crow Street, Dublin.

Taxis for Hire. Phone 768 Dublin; or write Stritch, 1 South Circular Road, Dublin.

Butter, Butter. No scarcity at Bailey's, only best Creamery stocked. Call early to avoid the Rush. Bailey, Phibsborough. Telephone—Drumcondra 13.

Slyne's Sale. Evening Gown in Shell Pink Georgette with Crystal Trimmings. Sale Price 8½ Gns. Slyne and Co., 71 Grafton Street.

If you wish to ascertain the purchasing power of a £1 Note to-day — visit Kellett's Household Linen Department. Cotton Sheets Double size 16/6 to 31/- per pair. Supreme value. Shop early.

No *certainly not. In answer to numerous enquiries Tylers do not stock re-constructed Army Boots at any of their Branches.*

10

Troubles

January 1919 was a month Mr Bloom would always remember. In common with most Dubliners, and most of the country, he looked forward to the advent of a new Ireland with excitement.

In the general election which followed the end of the Great War, Mr Bloom had voted for Sinn Fein — largely out of old loyalty to Arthur Griffith, even though the party now called Sinn Fein had little in common with the group who created that name in 1905.

So Mr Bloom took a day off work to go down to the Mansion House on 19 January to cheer in those Sinn Fein members who had been elected to the imperial parliament but who chose instead to constitute themselves as an independent body sitting in Dublin. Here at last was an Irish parliament, the long dreamed of outcome of the people's hopes, even if it was not in the old Parliament House on College Green, and even if it had been given a queer new name, the Dail. Mr Bloom had no feeling at all for the Irish language, but he suspected that he would have to get used to it in the future.

On the same day that the Dail first met the War of Independence, fought between the IRA and the Crown forces, broke out. The next two and a half years were to be dominated by the conflict, although Dublin was relatively unaffected — with a few notable exceptions.

But in those years after the Great War, when the unemployed ex-soldier was a common enough sight begging for a meal or a small job, it was the difficulty of earning a living that troubled people most. Bread and butter, more than blood and iron, were the pressing concerns of the day.

For Leopold Bloom this had meant, since 1902, the canvassing of advertisements for the columns of the *Freeman's Journal*. In his earlier years he had gone from job to job, mainly because he was forever falling out with his employers. But when Molly and he had settled into Eccles Street he had tried seriously to hold down the newspaper job. He was very much his own man in how he went about it, and it was largely that which made it attractive to him. The editor did not have much time for him, but then, Bloom reflected, if it were not for his advertisements there would be no paper.

He had often thought vaguely that some new opportunity would come along, perhaps in one of the new advertising agencies, which were now becoming so important in the commercial world. Hugh Boylan had worked for one in D'Olier Street, the Advertising Company Ltd., and while Boylan had been enamoured of Molly, Bloom had sounded him out on the chance of a job, but had been rebuffed. Boylan did not need Molly so badly that he would have to put up a salary for her husband. These agencies were no mere bill posters, but employed people who created the demand for new products. Business must advertise. Bloom, who had read up all the American salesmen's guides which Capel Street Public Library could provide, knew all about the theory of the thing. People often said he had some skill with a catchy jingle. But a sense of inertia, of paralysis almost, prevented him from exerting himself. This became more so after Molly's death. He was alright where he was.

The 'troubles', as they later came to be called, were a difficult time for Bloom. With all the uncertainty there was little business confidence and this made it hard to extract renewals from old advertisers. But he scraped along, as did the paper, for everyone was naturally anxious to read every detail of the events happening around them. Only when he read about it in the paper could Mr Bloom be certain of the facts of something he might have seen for himself.

One evening in January 1920 Bloom was waiting to meet Mick Doyle, one of the fellows from the *Evening Mail*, outside the Standard Hotel. The Standard was a temperance hotel which suited his total abstinence friend very well. The streets were crowded with people making their way home from work, many walking towards the railway station.

Bloom noticed a thickset man coming towards the hotel entrance, and then behind him, gaining on him, another man in a raincoat. A few yards from the door where he stood, Bloom saw the man behind draw a revolver and shoot the first man in the back. He swung round as he fell, but he must have been dead before he rolled over into the gutter. There were screams and shouts and people scattered across the road for fear of more flying bullets.

The man in the gutter was a police intelligence officer, the man behind one of the squad prowling the city at Michael Collins' behest to search out and eliminate these agents who threatened the freedom movement.

The pool of blood turned black under the gas lights. A doctor knelt by the man, but there was nothing to be done. In a few minutes an ambulance drew up and the corpse was wrapped in a blanket and driven away. It had taken only a few minutes. Bloom stumbled into the hotel in search of the toilet and threw up in a handbasin. The sight of calculated murder, seen face to face, was too much for him. When he came out Mick Doyle had arrived.

'I've been waiting ages for you, Bloom. God, you look ghastly man. What was all the excitement out there?'

'I've just had the privilege of witnessing an historic moment in Ireland's fight for freedom,' said Bloom. 'And now, my friend, whether you like it or not, I am going out to buy a drink, for me, if not for you.'

The policeman's name was Redmond, not that it seemed to matter much. This was only one of many shootings, murders and woundings in the city that year. On 20 December 1919 the IRA had even tried to assassinate Lord French, the Lord Lieutenant: they only just failed, with one of the attackers being killed. In January 1920 the local elections had been held and Sinn Fein had carried the day. By this time 'the troubles' were becoming serious. The Dail was suppressed, and on 23 February a curfew was imposed on Dublin. Mr Bloom found he had to stay indoors between midnight and five o'clock in the morning.

'Hardly affects me,' he said to his daughter. 'Who'd want to be about at those hours in any case?'

'At your age you should know better than to be lurking in the streets after ten anyway,' she replied.

During the summer nights the curfew was altered, relaxing the bar to three o'clock. But again in November the hours were increased to run from ten o'clock to five o'clock in the morning. During these long dark hours lorries rumbled through the city streets, searching out terrorists, the authorities claimed; in fact terrorising the civilian population, Sinn Fein claimed. These measures cut into the social life of the city, but in fact did little to affect the operations of the IRA. The struggle went on.

During these years Mr Bloom remained with his daughter and her family in Drumcondra. Her husband Jerry still maintained his links with the movement, even while continuing to work as a civil servant in the Department of Agriculture and Technical Instruction. But in this he was not unique. Many Nationalists who had fought in the Great War later became Republicans fighting with the IRA. Many 'Sinn Feiners', as the British would have called them, held positions in the Irish administration. Indeed it was rumoured that a large part of the success which Collins had in eliminating his 'enemies' was due to his network of informers high up in the administration. Jerry's links gave the family a feeling for the course of events which might have seemed mysterious to many.

At strange hours of the day or night the house would harbour visitors about whose identity Mr Bloom was often glad to be left in doubt. It did not do, in Dublin during 1920, to know too much. Sometimes, however, he could not help himself.

One morning in April he came down to find a group of young men seated at the kitchen table. At their head sat a large, domineering figure, devouring a huge helping of bacon, eggs and fried bread. Bloom knew at once who he was: the reputation of Michael Collins, the effective leader of the IRA, had preceded him. He had a reward of £10,000 on his head. It was hard to believe that he was not yet thirty. The object of constant British army searches, he always eluded them, talked his way past them and continued to cycle openly around Dublin. Collins had arrived the evening before on his bicycle and had slept the night in the small house. But he would not be there that night.

'Good morning,' said Collins cheerfully to Bloom, who

130

settled himself to his own breakfast. Then it was back to a busy conversation with his colleagues.

Bloom ate in silence. This contact with greatness was enough to unnerve him. Collins blew into houses with a gush of rural power which was unsettling to quiet civic souls, tossing the long neglected folds of a settled life into a new shape before he blew out again.

'No, no, the countryside is loyal to us and what the country feels today, the city feels tomorrow. We have them on the go and the touts are no longer a danger to us.' Nor were they. By now Collins' 'squad' had succeeded in eliminating the majority of informers and intelligence men like Redmond, the eyes and ears of British security.

Bloom saw in his memory that other leader, waving from the open window, his face pale with passion. The aristocrat. Now here was the man of the people, all ruthless energy and purpose.

All his life Bloom had hated violence. His father had been full of stories about the events of 1848 when he was a child. He had grown up fearing violence, knowing only too well what men with a good cause were capable of. He had admired men who had striven to improve the lot of Ireland through lawful means, who turned the constitution to their own gain. He had admired O'Connell and Parnell, not the Fenians or the Invincibles. Now here was the epitome of the Fenians, laughing over his breakfast; here was the man all Ireland admired; and here was a man Bloom feared. He saw the impatience of the revolutionary, and wondered what a man like this would be like in more settled times. Would fools be suffered gladly then? Would 'enemies' still be eliminated on street corners? In times of violence, the solution was easy. In peace, what might he be capable of?

Yet for the follower of Parnell, the admirer of Griffith, this was a memorable moment. There was no denying it: Collins was electric! He had taken on the imperial might of Britain and whether or not he was going to win, he had already made a better fight of it than any previous Irish revolutionary. Leaving after his meal, Collins shook hands with Jerry and nodded to Bloom.

'Thank you,' he said and was gone, looking neither left nor right as he rode down the street on his bicycle as if it had been his daily route to work for a decade.

131

During these troubled days Mr Bloom tried to go about his daily business as best he could. By now the *Freeman's Journal* was struggling, nor was the country's economy in good shape. The Great War had been an economic boon to Ireland, especially to the farmers. The revolution coincided with the post-war depression.

Making his way about a once peaceful city was now a risky affair. Road blocks and searches had become the accepted order of the day. After May 1920 the Black and Tans and the Auxiliaries, with their more forceful attitude towards keeping the king's peace, became a murderous menace. Even a harmless citizen like Mr Bloom would find himself stopped and questioned.

'Bloom? Is that an Irish name?' the officer asked at Mount Street Bridge.

'Oh yes, I was born here in Dublin.'

The officer looked him over with disdain.

'Sounds Jewish to me. Sure it isn't Jewish?'

'Well, yes, it is actually.'

'Then it can't be Irish. Who ever heard of an Irish Jew?' he asked the other soldiers. 'That'd be as odd as a generous Scotsman. It's a Bolshie jew name. I should run you in as a Red spy.'

So Bloom was held for questioning, and was bundled into the back of a lorry, which soon rattled off into the city. This, he thought fearfully, is how poor Sheehy-Skeffington died. Some lunatic like Bowen-Colthurst could do for me and none would be the wiser.

A green painted room with a single light bulb to illuminate its bare squalor. He sat on the hard chair and waited, watching with gathering unease the soldier guarding the door.

Then a senior officer arrived. Bloom explained that he was merely a humble employee of the *Freeman's Journal* (he knew an intelligent soldier like this would never tangle with anyone who could gain publicity for his sufferings within an hour.) No, he had no political views. No connections with Sinn Fein. The officer looked puzzled.

'Bloom. That's an odd name. Can't be many of your family in Dublin.'

Bloom agreed that Blooms were thin on the ground.

132

'I was wondering. I was at school with a Bloom. Where did you go to school?'

Bloom now looked more closely at the face before him. Yes indeed. Though changed by the years and the experiences of war, he could still see the features of the boy he had known as Michael Armstrong.

'I believe I can remember you,' said Bloom. 'Michael Armstrong, isn't it?'

'They called you mackeral didn't they? That was a long time ago. You were years ahead of me. You were friendly with that fellow Apjohn out in Crumlin. What became of him? He was an army man, I think.'

'He was killed. In the Boer War. At Modder River.'

Armstrong nodded.

'They're putting up a memorial in the school, you know. I had a note about it, looking for a sub. To the boys butchered in the War. There were a good number of them for a small place. I don't suppose many people remember about Modder River now, not after Mons. Here, come on out of this. I'll give you a drink. Dare say you need one.'

So Bloom was released. He had needed the drink, though the officer's chat about old school days and their jolly scrapes seemed at odds with the present circumstances. His brief absence went unremarked.

The year passed. Little more than twelve months after he had met Collins, Bloom was crossing over O'Connell Bridge when he was astonished by the sound of gunfire and billows of smoke drifting over the Liffey from the Custom House. His view was obscured by the railway bridge, and a military cordon was already in place. The next day the newspaper revealed that the IRA had attempted a major stroke by attacking and attempting to destroy the centre of the British local government administration in Ireland. It was a daring raid, and might have shown that they could do what they liked. But as 126 of them were surrounded and detained the affair was a fiasco.

In fact the IRA was near the end of its tether. In Dublin these arrests broke the organisation. Elsewhere, arms and ammunition were in short supply. When the truce came in July, it was a relief not only to the general population, but to the tiny bands of men who had been fighting the British.

133

Bloom and the family in Wellpark Avenue were delighted. That summer was a remarkable one for the whole country. For the first time in years people could go about without being in fear of armed men or curfews. All through the autumn and early winter, Irish delegations, led first by de Valera, then by Arthur Griffith and Collins, negotiated with the British in London. Home Rule was no longer enough. Eventually, at the start of December, the Anglo-Irish treaty was signed, giving dominion status to the twenty-six counties of the Catholic south. (The six largely Protestant counties of the North had already declared their determination to remain in the United Kingdom, thus effecting the partition of Ireland.) Like the Christmas of 1891, that of 1921 saw festive tables hot with debate, on the merits of the treaty, the nature of the new oath of allegiance, the value of dominion status in the light of the republican ideal. The dream of 1916 had come face to face with the reality of 1921.

From the beginning, Bloom had been in favour of the settlement. He was of an older generation, anyway, and hankered after that form of government which was closer to Home Rule. Some of the young republican zealots disturbed him, with their vision of a Gaelic-speaking, rural nation 'uncontaminated' by outside influences. Bloom was temperamentally inclined to side against zealots, any zealots. Besides, he reasoned that control of finance, defence and law and order were the real badges of freedom, and Ireland was to have these. Why, there was even to be a separate flag! Eventually, the Dail accepted the treaty by a small majority and de Valera, who was personally anti-treaty, resigned the leadership. He was replaced by Arthur Griffith, author of *The Resurrection of Hungary*.

Jerry McCarthy, too, was pro-treaty, but only just, and largely out of admiration for Collins. He was sorry to see de Valera step down.

'It's a sad day when comrades fall out in this way.'

'Ah, where everyone makes everything a matter of principle, there's never any room for manoeuvre,' said Bloom. 'De Valera seems to have a very rigid view of things.'

'I'm sure that given time he would accept their view. But it all seems forced on us by the British.'

'You know Jerry it may well have been inevitable. You

134

think this is all new. But look at what happened after Parnell. Splits and rows. Strife seems to come naturally to us.'

Wherever he went in Dublin Bloom was now aware of the armed camps into which the old movement had divided. Across the country the IRA garrisons which had taken over from the British divided for or against the Treaty. Incidents occurred; there were armed clashes. Then in April 1922, the Four Courts building in Dublin was seized by opponents of the Treaty. Was it to be Easter Week again? A sense of foreboding crept over the city, as though the worst was yet to come.

'Will it come to a fight, Jerry?' asked Bloom one evening as he read the day's developments in the *Evening Mail.*

'It can't be avoided,' said Jerry, with resignation. 'It has become a matter of authority. To revolt against the British was one thing. To stand out against a settlement accepted by the majority is another thing.'

'God help us, Jerry, a civil war would be a terrible thing. Look at Russia or Germany. We'll have Nansen over here yet bringing us aid in another famine if we don't watch out.'

'Oh father, don't talk like that. Can't we have some bright talk instead of all this politics and gloomy old chat,' asked Milly.

'Now Milly, it's serious enough, but perhaps we could have a little less of it while the boy is around.'

Rudy looked up from his boiled egg.

'Will you tell me about Sinbad's adventures, granda, when I go to bed?'

'I will Rudy. All about Sinbad's adventures, and the Valley of the Diamonds and the Giant Roc Bird.'

The other giant roc which had been hovering over Dublin finally plunged down and struck. On Monday 26 June, men from the Four Courts in need of cars to escape to the North raided Henderson's dealership and took sixteen vehicles. The Republican officer in charge of the raid was arrested and put into Mountjoy Jail as a car thief. The Four Courts garrison retaliated by seizing General 'Ginger' O'Connell. Dubliners had been patient with fellow patriots — car thieves were another matter. An ultimatum was issued to the garrison by the government. No reply was made.

On Wednesday morning Bloom woke with a start. In the

distance could be heard, every fifteen minutes, the heavy thump of artillery. What was happening? Had the British, vexed beyond endurance by the murder in London of General Sir Henry Wilson by two IRA men, returned to take care of the problem in their own way?

But no, it was the government troops firing on the Four Courts. This was the start of a week's fighting in Dublin, which was more intense even than the Rising. It ended with another quarter of O'Connell Street burned out, the Four Courts blown up, and the Public Record Office ruined. It was an appalling affair, which left many people stunned. The political simplicity of the fight against the traditional enemy had now been replaced by divided and ambiguous attitudes. Only a small hard core of men could long preserve an innocence of vision to pretend they were fighting for the Republic declared in 1916.

Day by day Bloom would follow in the censored papers the progress of the war. Once again the daily round had been disturbed, shops burned, homes wrecked, but the *Freeman's Journal* still appeared. And still needed his ads. So Bloom worked on getting about as best he could. After the first intense week, the fighting was mainly in the country, indeed mostly in the south west, long a staunch Republican area. For Jerry this was a hard time, seeing what was happening on his native heath, but he still retained his loyalty to Cork through his admiration for Collins.

Cork City was taken by a sudden attack from the sea. What remained of the Republican army moved further west, into Muskerry and Kerry. The pressure of events on the government was very great, an intolerable burden on men who had laboured so long to achieve their country's freedom.

Bloom had gone down to the shop to buy his morning paper. But before he could say one word, Mrs Byrne blurted out:

'Oh Mr Bloom, isn't it dreadful? What will become of us now, with Arthur Griffith gone?'

And there it was, in the headline of the paper. *Griffith Dead.* He had collapsed and died at St Vincent's Nursing Home in Leeson Street the previous day. It was 13 August,

136

a hot, weary month.

Bloom thought about his meeting with Arthur Griffith, ever so many years ago now, when he had told him all about the men of Hungary and had inspired Griffith (as he had always fondly believed) to write the famous book which led to the creation of Sinn Fein. All the other talks they had had later.

'Granda, will you take me down to the Gardens?' Rudy begged, and the old man sadly obliged. One still owed the future to the young.

'Come on then, Rudy, get your cap and we'll go. And I'll tell you more about Sinbad too.'

Arthur Griffith had talked of sailing home from South Africa and coming into Zanzibar, and the heavy scent of the cloves coming out on the breeze to meet them. Of the white houses in the hot sun, and the black men working on the quays and the Arabs in long robes with curved knives at their waists: just like the *Arabian Nights* he had said. This had been one of Sinbad's ports. And now Griffith was dead.

Four days later, Griffith's state funeral was an occasion of solemn pomp, displaying the intention of the new government to create the full dignity of statehood. Bloom and Jerry took the boy down the road to see the cortege pass. Bloom was deeply saddened. So long ago he had pointed out to Molly the small, vital man, bouncing along on the balls of his feet with that queer walk of his, as a 'coming man'. Now the coming man was gone. In those days Sinn Fein had been a party of non-violence, but now the physical force boys had taken over.

There at the head of the mourners was Michael Collins with General Richard Mulcahy. In his uniform he seemed a larger man than he had over the breakfast table. His face had filled out, and he looked impressively virile. The crowd would have cheered him had it not been a funeral. For many of them this was the first sight of the legendary leader, and whispers of admiration followed him.

Mr Bloom had hardly absorbed the impact of Arthur Griffith's death when the more dreadful news of Collins' death in an ambush in West Cork reached Dublin. His own had struck him down. Jerry was dismayed, sickened at the horror of it. Bloom felt for his son-in-law.

137

'Ah Jerry we don't deserve to have great men. Look what they did to Parnell, and now to Griffith and Collins. What a nation!'

A few days later, after Collins' own funeral had passed into Glasnevin, Bloom saw chalked up on a wall in town *Move over Mick — Make room for Dick.* But Mulcahy survived. The Civil War now entered a new and more terrible phase, with terror and assassination freely used on both sides. But it was clear that public sympathy was against the republicans and for the government.

The shock of loss had numbed people. They had had enough. Everywhere there was support for the Free State, as the country was to be called, which showed itself in a new election. Bloom voted once again for the government, now led by the somewhat colourless William Cosgrave. But it was time for colourless men. They had seen enough of heroes.

'And now Jerry, we will have to set to work, I suppose. No more excitements. We can return to the thrill of ordinary life.'

'Like watching girls in Stephen's Green,' said his son-in-law with a slightly disagreable leer.

True enough, thought Bloom. He had long found watching women and girls more interesting than public affairs. If the freedom of Ireland was the freedom to watch girls well and good. Bloom had always had a masher mentality. He wondered about Jerry McCarthy sometimes. Were there no mashers in Cork?

Bloom had not much liked Jeremiah Florence McCarthy when he had married Milly. He could not see what she saw in him. But over the troubled years, living closely with them through the Great War, and the lost child, and the disturbances, he had come to see the better qualities of the young Cork man. Jerry too had changed. The brash young antisemite had not survived the man. A much sobered husband and father now faced the new Ireland with his wife and children.

Bloom had enjoyed his years with them, but felt that now, perhaps, they had their own lives to live. It was time for him to move on again.

1923

Would kind R.C. woman adopt very handsome Baby boy, just two years old, respectable parents, without fee; no roomkeepers accepted.

Ask for Dublin's Best Stout. Mountjoy. Insist on getting it. Take no other. Any difficulty in procuring same can be got over by writing or telephoning the Brewery.

Important News for Dublin. Mons. Le Mayen, from Paris, French Eyesight Specialist, Opthalmic Optician, 45 Years Experience. Impossible to Stay Longer. Saturday Positively Last Day. At Shaw Ltd., Jewellers, Corner Earl Street and O'Connell Street.

Sherwood's Linoleum. Best and Cheapest Largest stock in the Trade. 55 Middle Abbey Street. Open on Wednesdays.

Because I Love You So, 3s. record, only obtainable at "The Gramophone Stores". Johnson's Court, Grafton Street, Dublin.

The Seven Ages of Woman No. 3: The Flapper. She will probably never be happier than she is in these merry days when everyone about her ministers to her pleasure. Troubles may come all too soon, but to-day she is happy, carefree, full of the joy of life. And not the least of her pleasures is a plentiful supply of N.K.M. Irish Cream Toffee. 7½d. a qrt.

First Church of Christ, Scientist, Dublin (a branch of the Mother Church, the First Church of Christ, Scientist, in Boston, Mass.) 35 Molesworth Street.

Mr John McCormack, Famous Tenor, to Arrive in Dublin Tomorrow.

There is no better way of making Money out of Money, than by a regular investment in Irish Free State Savings Certificates. "Guaranteed by the Irish Nation."

All-Army Championships. 1923. August 25th Sept 2nd. Dublin's Biggest Sporting event.

Important to Mothers. Every mother who values the Health and Cleanliness of Her Child should use Harrison's Pomade. One application kills all Nits and Vermin, beautifies and strengthens hair. Tins 6d. & 1/-. Sold by all chemists.

Sinn Fein Election Fund. Subscriptions should be sent to Dr Con Murphy, Director of Finance, or to Mrs Cathal Brugha, Hon. Treasurer, 23 Suffolk Street, Dublin.

Revival of Irish Industry is a Mighty Task. Yet it can be Accomplished. Begin! By using Irish-made Paper. Do Your Part. See that your friends do theirs. Remember the words — "United Effort". Remember the Object, "Irish Prosperity". The North of Ireland Paper Mill Co., Ltd, Ballyclare & Larne, Antrim.

11

Bloom and the New Ireland

For Leopold Bloom, as for Ireland, the first years of the Free
State marked the beginning of a new life. The *Freeman's
Journal*, for so long the paper that had represented the older
Irish nationalism, gave up the unequal economic struggle,
and died in December 1924. Its title was absorbed into the
Irish Independent, founded in 1907 by William Martin
Murphy. But by then Mr Bloom had already left the *Freeman*
for pastures new.

His son-in-law, having risen dramatically through the ranks
of the civil service, was able to use his influence with 'the
new people' to get Mr Bloom a position as an insurance
clerk with the New Ireland Assurance Company in 1923.
Mr Bloom was then able to joke about having a stake in
'the New Ireland'. The company had been founded as part
of the economic 'new Ireland' envisaged by such men as
Collins and Griffith.

The job brought Bloom into contact with the people who
were now running the country. Throughout the business
community there had been little real change, but there
was a general feeling that there would be. Or as his friend
at work, Sean Purcell, expressed it to Bloom: 'The Pro-
testants and the Freemasons won't have it all their own
way from now on!'

Catholics felt they had been excluded for so long and
were now reaching out to grasp what had been denied them.
This was not, of course, really true. What had the late Mr
William Martin Murphy represented if not Catholic economic
power, Bloom enquired. 'Well then, let there be more Murphys
in the future', said Purcell, slamming the lid of a box file to
preclude further discussion. 'Your man Bloom' was always
arguing.

Bloom decided he would mark his new job by taking new lodgings. He went to live in a house run with commendable grace by a Mrs Quinn in Clonliffe Road. Bloom preferred now to live his own life (even at the age of 58), but at the same time he had come to enjoy his grandson's company so much that this break made their meetings all the more entertaining. Clonliffe Road was near enough to Wellpark Avenue, but far enough away to leave Bloom feeling free. With the boy he began to explore and experience the city again, discovering as he did whole new aspects of urban life. With the boy it was a matter of demonstrating the old delights of the city streets as he had known them since the 1870s, since he had first begun to walk to school in fact, at little more than Rudy's present age. But in addition to the landmarks of the past were novelties which delighted him. Among these was greyhound racing.

Mr Bloom had never really been a sporting man, not since he had been a runner at school. He had witnessed, with distaste, the growing interest of everyone around him in sport to the exclusion of all else. The Gaelic Athletic crowd, who made Sundays so noisy around his area of the city, had been bad enough. Now there was a spreading enthusiasm for Soccer and even for Rugby — though that seemed to be the exclusive interest of middle-class professional Dublin.

Then 'the dogs' arrived. Horse racing had been a thing which had entertained Mr Bloom. In their day he and Molly had enjoyed many an afternoon at Leopardstown and Fairyhouse with their friends. That had been fun. But 'the dogs' were a passion.

Racing greyhounds made their appearance first at Manchester in 1926, arriving in Ireland in 1927. The National Greyhound Racing Company (everything in those days was 'national'), opened a course around the playing field in Shelbourne Park, a soccer ground. The first meeting was on 18 May 1927, and curiosity took Mr Bloom along.

Here, between the gasworks and the docks, the park was crowded, both inside and outside. Even from the cheap seats he was able to have a good view of the track and to lay a bet or two. Oddly enough there always seemed to be a greater number of women, all eagerly interested in the actual dogs running in the meet. Bets were taken by the familiar crew of bag men who also appeared at Leopardstown to take the punters' money. That first night Mr Bloom, by the fortuitous nature of all gambling by the ignorant, went home with new gained cash in his pocket. The dogs were elevated in his mind to a complete delight; there was nothing like them. Even when, on later visits, he lost, the atmosphere of the crowd and the brief, intense excitement of the races seemed sufficient compensation.

Bloom, like many a man rising sixty, found himself looking as much to the past as the future. Often in the course of his work he would pass the high, black railings of the High School and cast an appraising eye over the old buildings. Then one day at the office, while glancing through the *Irish Times*, he saw an announcement of an Old School Dinner for past pupils of the High School. He recalled Michael Armstrong and his talk during the dark days of the troubles, and thought it would be curious to see how their *alma mater* was adapting to the new way of life in Ireland. He wrote off for tickets, and on the appointed night arrived at Harcourt Street in a hired evening suit and black tie.

He found that there were now few familiar faces among the crowd milling about the foyer. But then he thought he recognised the face of Owen Goldberg. Goldberg too remembered him. It had been more than three decades since they had even seen each other.

'What are you doing these days, Bloom?' Goldberg asked.

'Oh, I'm in insurance,' said Bloom airily.

'A fine thing. I'm in South Africa now, you know, in the diamond business. Not in a big way, of course. Wonderful country, South Africa.' He lowered his head towards Bloom.

'A fine country for people of our persuasion, you know.'

For a wild moment Bloom thought he meant the Masons, but then he realised he was talking about the Jews.

'I am sure of it. Things are not so bad here though. At least not as bad as I imagine many of our school fellows thought they were going to be.'

They passed into dinner. Grace was recited by a colonial bishop beneath walls still hung with the portraits of famous old boys and imperial heroes. After dinner the headmaster made a speech welcoming them home, so to speak. He too took as his theme change and continuity. And then the toasts were proposed.

'The King.'

'The King.'

Bloom paused, only for a moment, and then out of politeness, raised his glass. Their gods were no longer his. These comfortable, middle-aged men were being washed into a backwater by the tide of history. Perhaps in time their sons would be able to paddle out. But for now, they were truly up the creek.

Leaving, he made a tentative arrangement with Owen Goldberg to dine with him at the Kildare Street Club, before he returned to South Africa. But he never took up the invitation. It would have been just too much for him to carry through.

This nostalgia for the lost corners of his youth took him at the Passover of 5685 (which is to say Easter 1924) to attend the service in the synagogue in Adelaide Road. There he was seated as a stranger, which was appropriate when he thought how long it was since he had even heard Hebrew recited. The soberly dressed congregation, among whom he recognised so many familiar faces of jewellers and dentists, sat in solemn attention. His poor father, in his last years, had halfheartedly tried to take up again the practice of his ancestral faith. It had been too late for him, who had been brought up in the ways of Israel; for his son, who had not been taught at all, it was impossible to go back. Within little more than a generation, the members of this community had come from Europe and were now fully part of Irish life, yet they had kept the abiding strength of their ancient faith. Bloom had no faith, and doubts about his fatherland. He noticed as he came away that they were collecting for an extension fund. Whatever notes he had in his wallet he stuffed into the box.

Another event in 1924 which Mr Bloom could not resist attending was the unveiling in College Green on 11 November of a huge celtic cross as a memorial to the Irish dead in the Great War. Eventually the cross would be taken over to France, but for now it stood defiantly in the middle of the city, to the anger of many republicans.

144

'What sort of business is this, these poppy sellers and war memorials to foreign armies,' Sean Purcell remarked to Bloom as they made their way back from lunch one day.

'But surely in Dublin many thousands have dead relatives they wish to remember.'

'They should remember those who died for Ireland.'

'But for them, they did die for Ireland, over 60,000 Irishmen all told. I believe there were less than 2,000 men out in Easter Week.'

His colleague snorted. This was to be taken as a gesture as final as slamming the lid of his box file.

That summer Sean had been entertained by the spectacle of the Tailteann Games, the native Irish Olympics as some people called them. This curious display, with prizes for poets as well as athletes, was all part of an anxious effort to 'gaelicise' the public and sporting life of the country.

The disappearance of the Royal Irish Constabulary and the Dublin Metropolitan Police were an inevitable part of the settlement. So too was the radical colour change in public life. Wherever things had been royal red they were now re-painted Irish green. Telegrams and official documents, pillar boxes and public utilities. New notes and coins would follow in due course.

Dublin was becoming a modern city, with trams, cinemas, motor cars and dance halls. The city, Sean told him, was dance mad. The young were totally preoccupied, it seemed, with jazzing and the talkies. For Mr Bloom, reared in the gentler tastes of Victoria's reign, jazz had no appeal. The priests said it was brothel music and it sounded like it. If Mr Bloom required music he would sit at home with his phonograph, playing the recordings of Count McCormack.

He had first heard McCormack sing in August 1903, when the young man fresh from Athlone had shared a platform with other young performers. Bloom had often wondered what had become of others who had sung that day, why their talents had not developed as McCormack's had. Mysterious things, art and talent.

Many long winter evenings he could now while away in his lodgings with songs that had enchanted Molly and him in the days of their youth, love's old sweet songs.

Just a song at twilight, when the lights are low
And the flick'ring shadows softly come and go.
Tho' the heart be weary, sad the day and long,
Still to us at twilight comes
Love's old song, comes love's old sweet song.

But of all the novelties of the day, Mr Bloom found the cinema quite the most enchanting. To plunge out of the daylight into the darkness, illuminated only with a screen on which passed shadows of life, always excited him. He had gone with Molly to the first real cinema in Dublin; now he often went with Rudy on Saturday afternoons.

To both man and boy the flickers were an engrossing romance. The great stars of the modern firmament shone brightly in their brief passages. Charlie Chaplin had entertained them for years, William S. Hart thrilled, Mary Pickford enchanted. But for Mr Bloom Douglas Fairbanks was the man. The swiftly moving scenes from his swashbuckling adventures removed him completely from the confines of everyday life, from the drudgery of the office and the weary daily round.

Saturday by now had its own routine. At lunch time he would meet Rudy, fresh from school. Sometimes they would take themselves off to some particular place: Christ Church, the Natural History Museum, the Botanic Gardens. Other days it would be to see some film selected with care from the entertainment column in the *Evening Mail*. Following this they would have high tea in the DBC or some other restaurant. And afterwards home by tram to Drumcondra, where there would be cocoa for the boy and a glass of sherry wine, as Milly called it, for her father. Then a brisk walk back to Clonliffe Road.

During 1925 Dubliners watched with interest the repairing of the main streets with asphalt, concrete and wooden blocks instead of the old cobblestones. That same year saw the extension out into the suburbs of buses of the Tramway Company and of many other smaller firms. On some routes there was fierce competition between them for passengers, and buses would race each other to the stops to pick up passengers. That year, too, taxi cabs of the modern kind were licensed to run in Dublin for the first time, bringing to an end the era of the horse-drawn cabs.

These things, Mr Bloom realised, were symptoms of a growing city. A census in 1926 showed 316,471 people now lived in the metropolitan area. In a changing city Mr Bloom was only too glad to find some unchanging features, such as the Mater Hospital, the National Library, and the girls selling flowers under the Pillar.

In his old age (as he was coming to think of it) Mr Bloom was spending more time in pubs than he had once done, finding the habitués a relaxed company in which to while the time away pleasantly. The drinking hours were as regulated as they had once been liberal, but this made little difference. At any hour of the day, he could still find someone in a pub. But then with the advent of the lounge bar, even the arcane drinking habits of the city began to change. These were places where you would see young people, yes girls even, drinking some smart new drink. Mr Bloom sometimes despaired of the younger generation. Though young Rudy, the companion of his walks, was a bright spark.

One completely new place which Bloom and Rudy visited was Leinster House during a session of the Dail. This great mansion had once been the residence of the Dukes of Leinster — indeed the open space before it, facing Merrion Square, had been known as the Duke's Lawn to the children who played there before it was closed to them. The house itself had been the headquarters of the Royal Dublin Society until 1925, when they moved out to Ballsbridge and the Dail deputies moved in.

They passed in giving their names to the gate keepers. From the visitors' gallery they could look down on the Dail in session. To Mr Bloom it came as something of a surprise. He had long been used to the public style of Irish politics, the impassioned orator ranting from the street-corner platform, the crowd roaring and jeering, shaking their fists or heckling. But below him now the benches were only half-full, the deputies reading over their green order papers, and rising to put their questions, in Irish as often as in English. More surprising were the party leaders. Mr Cosgrave had the sober appearance of a bank manager; he was quite unlike the imperious Parnell or the vital Redmond. Perhaps

147

this augered well in its own way. Across the Dail sat de Valera, impassive and gaunt. In the past he had made fiery and provocative speeches and doubtless he would again. Throwing off the last entanglements of the Civil War, he had finally brought his party into the Dail in 1927. Soon he might well be leader of the country. Gazing down on this scene, and answering his grandson's questions, Mr Bloom brooded on the fate reserved for leaders. The dream of his youth had been to see Parnell take his seat in the Old Parliament House in College Green, and then rise to address the nation in the style of Grattan.

'Yes, Rudy, that is Mr Cosgrave, and the other man is Mr de Valera. No, his name is Spanish, they say, but he's Irish now. Yes, Rudy, the other man is the leader of the country.'

He sighed. Poor Parnell, his poor dead king.

Coming out they gazed, as Bloom often had in the past, on the huge statue of Queen Victoria in front of Leinster House. 'Ireland's Revenge' they called it in Dublin, where it was thought to be remarkably ugly. On the plinth were figures representing Peace and War. It had been unveiled to the ribald wonder of the city on 15 February 1908. Bloom doubted that it would be allowed to stay where it was much longer.

The statue was the work of John Hughes, for whom Molly had once posed in the nude. Hughes began all his statues from the nude. Molly had been, what was it, a Madonna for a church in the West of Ireland. Bloom wondered who Hughes had found to strip off for the part of Queen Victoria.

1929

Insure Nationally. Insurance is a secure stand-by . . . but insure nationally *with our firm. There is a dual purpose in so doing. You get the many advantages of a firm built through the confidence of the public. We invest in Irish concerns. By doing business with us you're helping Irish industries and firms. New Ireland Assurance Co., Ltd., 12 Dawson Street.*

Travel by Bus. You can get a Carmel *every few minutes on any of the following routes. Sandymount, Terenure, Rialto, Donnybrook. Offices: 204 Pearse Street, Dublin.*

Michael Sheenan, Confidential Enquiry Agent, Late Detective Department, Dublin Castle. Residence, 38 Edenvale Road, Ranelagh, Dublin. Enquiries of every kind undertaken on moderate terms.

W. O'Mahony, late of Lenehan & Son, Castle Street. Leather factor. Moroccos, Roans, Skivers, Suedes. Chamois and Motor Linings. Also Book-Cloth, Web, Glue, Buckles Eyelets and Gut. 65 Capel Street, Dublin.

1929 wil see a new prosperity dawn in Ireland. And increased spending power means new kinds of printed jobs. *Versatility is essential to modern printers. Perfect versatility — the ability to handle any work, new or original, without strain or worry — is the great asset of printers who use the "Monotype".*

Picture Frame Makers C. Webb (E. Buchalter, Prop.) Wholesale and Retail Picture Frame Manufacturer and Gilder. Over 35 years established. 4 Crampton Quay, Dublin.

Money is scarce. Make the most of it when you buy your food. Get the best provisions at the most reasonable Price. You can depend upon good value if you buy your food from Martin Murphy.

Nation Builders Rich Cream Fresh Butter. New-laid eggs. Ireland's best can always be had at the Monument Creameries.

Irish Enterprise established Guineys of Talbot Street, Dublin. Irish Capital backs it. An Irishman — Denis Guiney — is Sole Proprietor. Irish Goods of the Highest Quality can be bought at Guineys cheaper than at any other store in the world. Guiney's, 79 & 80 Talbot Street, Dublin.

12

Gibraltar

The Levanter was hanging out over the peak of the Rock as the ship came in from the Atlantic to dock in Gibraltar. No sooner was he ashore than Mr Bloom became aware of the heavy lethargic atmosphere which this covering of cloud (unique to the promontory) brought to the little cluster of streets and roads which huddled along the shore under the steep slope of the peak. Sweet, sensuous and languorous, it seemed to him to explain a lot about his late wife.

Having retired and received, as well as a portion of his income as a pension, a large lump sum, Mr Bloom had given long thought to the spending of this windfall. A holiday seemed to be the best scheme, but where to go? London or Hungary attracted him, even Paris with its gay reputation. But then it occurred to him that a visit to the childhood haunts of Molly on the distant and exotic Rock of Gibraltar would really be the trip of a lifetime. He was to leave Ireland for the first time, at the age of sixty-three.

A journey from Dublin to Gibraltar was in itself an adventure. For, of course, there was no direct route. Mr Bloom had to take the Irish Mail to London and then go down to Southampton, from where an Indian boat gave him a passage to the town of Gibraltar. Unfamiliar sights and scenes assailed his senses all the way, leaving him with only a confused impression of change and speed. When he reached Gibraltar he needed a rest!

The Levanter was a cloud brought by the east wind, a wind which for centuries had blown into Gibraltar the various races of the East, the Jews, Moors, Indians, Maltese. But Mr Bloom was there as a mere tourist — an explorer in search of the past, the lost youth of his dead wife. While

151

on the boat out he had noted down, in so far as he was still able to recall them all, the stories which old Tweedy, her father, had told him, and the very few things which Molly herself had let slip. She had been quiet enough about her past, certainly, enough to add to these brief recollections the spice of mystery.

When they had first met he had not been much concerned with the history of the Tweedys. But then he had been surprised to learn the history of her mother and later that of Lieutenant Mulvey. Were there, he often wondered now, other things he did not know? Her memories, the essence of her past, could never be his. But he could try and recapture a very little bit of it by visiting the scenes of her childhood.

His first task was to find a cheap hotel, and this he soon did, with the customary aid of a taxi driver, who took him to a small place in Irishtown. Despite its name, this was not (as in Ireland) the 'native quarter' but a street in which Irish soldiers and their various women had once lived.

'From Ireland', said the man behind the desk. 'Then you'll feel at home in Irishtown, eh Senor?'

'I suppose so', said Mr Bloom, signing the register with an unaccustomed flourish.

'A holiday, eh', the man continued, naturally curious about what could bring such a person as Mr Bloom, clearly not a businessman or a civil servant, to Gibraltar at that season of the year.

'In a way, yes,' said Mr Bloom. 'You see my wife was born here, and being retired, I thought it might be fun to visit Gibraltar — having heard so much about it, you know, from her when she was alive.'

'Born on Gibraltar?' the man repeated. 'She was one of us? Or no, she would naturally have been one of the garrison.'

'Yes, that's right. Her father was a major named Tweedy. Oh this was all a long time ago, you know. But still. . . .'

'Ah senor, it is a pious thing indeed. I hope only that your piety will have its proper reward.'

And so Mr Bloom took his keys and went up to his room. While small and cramped, it was adequate. The hotel having no dining room, he then strolled out in search of somewhere to lunch. Passing a tourist shop, he stepped in and bought a

152

small pamphlet which gave him a short account of the town's history as well as a map which would help him find his way around. Over his lunch of wine and cheese, he took his bearings.

Here running down the slope of the Rock from the original station at the top of Willis's Road was the line of the Moorish wall. He remembered Molly mentioning that. And below it were the Alameda Gardens, which he would also have to visit. The road from there ran out to Europa Flats where the light on Europa Point winked away into the nights.

But if he were to discover anything about events of the 1870s he would have to begin at the library. So, his lunch finished, he walked along Water Port Street and turned up towards the Town Range Barracks, where the garrison library was situated. There the librarian explained that for a small fee he could make use of the library, seeing that his intentions were, so to speak, of a literary not to say academic nature.

The young librarian produced for him a run of the *Gibraltar Directory* covering the years the Tweedys had passed on the Rock, and Mr Bloom settled down with the red cloth-bound volumes to see what he could discover.

As he turned over the pages a picture emerged of a very different era. The long lists at the beginning of the volumes: the Roja family, the government of the day, the temporary commanders of the garrison — it was material familiar to Mr Bloom from his time on *Thom's Dublin Directory*, when he too had to scan such lists and make the annual changes. But it was with amusement he noted the address of the governor and his staff: The Convent and the Cottage, Europa. That would never have been allowed in Ireland!

On the Rock the military and their civilian confreres had established a thoroughly Victorian way of life with their clubs, the Calpe Hunt, Yacht Club and Lawn Tennis.

When he had looked through them, Mr Bloom returned the books to the desk. He explained his purpose and said he had hoped to find out a little about the life of the Tweedys without the labour of going through old papers and so on. The librarian thought for a moment.

'Now I think I might be able to help you. There is an old fellow, of, oh, about eighty or so who lives down in Engineer's Lane, with his daughter. He is said to be a wonderful fund of old gossip, you know what I mean, the sort of things that do not get into the papers. Call again tomorrow and I will have his address for you.'

'That is really very good of you. Just what I need.'

It was now late afternoon when Mr Bloom came out of the library. Consulting his map to orientate himself, he made his way back down to the hotel. Having freshened up he set off to explore the evening life of the town.

He walked out through the South Town to look over the Moorish Wall. This, he learnt from his pamphlet and the long passage in the Gibraltar guidebook, was all that remained of the stately palace and fortress built after the Moslem conquest.

Here, it came back to him, was where Molly had walked out with her young Lieutenant Mulvey, that sailor who had hardly time to kiss her before he was on his way again. She had been, what? fifteen in that year. He puzzled over it, probably so like her own daughter at that age, if he could remember her. That strain of dark Spanish blood, Arab blood perhaps, the sensuous heritage of the hot desert and cool harem quarters.

Beyond the wall were the Alameda Gardens. Here in the milder evening hours before dinner the people would wander in the walks talking with their friends. Often a band was on hand, the music drifting through the trees. The gardens were planted in terraces with trees and shrubs, luxuriant and lush to the eye with a profusion of garish geraniums. At the head of a flight of steps on a marble pillar stood a bust of General Elliot, and elsewhere a bust of the Duke of Wellington.

Mr Bloom settled down on a seat and watched the families going by and admired the pretty girls with their dark eyes and hair, their tempting olive skin. Spanish types, they recalled the bevy of girls in Matt Dillon's house in the old days.

Harassed by a sudden surge of memories, Mr Bloom decided it was time to seek out his dinner. Descending into Main Street, he wandered along inspecting such menus as were displayed outside the cafés, selecting at last one from which came a tempting aroma of grilling fish. In this he was wise, for anything else would have been almost uneatable. But the fish, fresh from the sea, bought that morning in the market, and served with a garlic and tomato sauce, could not have been better. With this he ordered, and drank, a complete bottle of a Spanish wine, a Valdepenos. He began to feel he might call himself a traveller, so far was he removed from what could be considered ordinary fare in Dublin.

And afterwards, back through the narrow streets to his hotel and the welcome peace of his bed, the sounds of cicadas in the trees through the open window.

'Ah yes, Mr Bloom. That address. I have it here.' The young librarian hunted among the papers on his desk and produced a small card on which was scribbled a name and address:

Mr Michael Nulty
4 Engineer's Lane.

and at the bottom 'lives with his daughter, Senora Gonzales.'

'And where is that situated', Mr Bloom asked, pointing to the address. The librarian gave him directions, and marked the street on his small tourist map. Thus prepared, Mr Bloom set out in search of the past.

He soon found the street, and the right house. He rang the bell beside a slip of card on which was typed Gonzales and under it in ink Nulty. Clearly Mrs Gonzales' father had frequent visitors.

The door was opened by a woman of about forty-five, with a large overflowing figure. The Spanish type.

'Senora Gonzales?' asked Mr Bloom, raising his hat.

'Yes', she replied in an English voice broken down by long years of speaking Spanish.

'I wish to speak with your father. It was suggested to me at the garrison library that he might be able to help me, to tell me about people living in Gibraltar in the 1870s.'

'Ah, you are English. Come in.'

'Thank you. No. Irish. Not quite the same thing.'

'No, of course not. My father is always the Irishman, but we are nearly all Britishers on Gibraltar. Come this way please.'

She led him up the open stairs to the apartment on the second floor. On an overstuffed armchair by the windows opening out onto the balcony sat an old man reading that morning's edition of the *Gibraltar Chronicle*.

'A visitor for you father,' said Senora Gonzales, and retired into the back part of the flat from which there was already creeping the subtle smells of lunch preparation.

The man in the chair looked up and Mr Bloom hurried across the room to introduce himself and explain the purpose of his visit.

'So you think I can help you. Well now, in what way would that be possible?'

'I am interested in hearing something, anything, about what life was like in Gibraltar. Especially anything about a Major Tweedy and his daughter Marion'.

'And for why?'

'Well you see,' Mr Bloom hesitated, as if it were necessary almost to apologise for the fact, 'I married Molly in Dublin, where they went to live afterwards. I'm on a bit of a holiday, like, to see what I can learn about the past. She's dead now. Dead some nineteen years.'

'Well', said Mr Nulty, folding away his paper, and settling himself in his chair. 'We can't dig up the past without having a small something in hand.'

He called out something in Spanish and almost at once his daughter came out with a tray, clearly already prepared, on which were some olives, a bottle of wine and two glasses. Mr Nulty passed him a full glass, and raised his own in toast.

'Salud'.

'Your health.'

'Well now, the old days. It's all changed now, anyone will tell you that. But by God we had some fine times when we were young. You know about old Tweedy. I recall him, but I mind he wasn't a major. Let me think now — he had a daughter right enough, by some Spanish woman. Let me think.'

The old man's mind lapsed back over the decades while he gazed out of the window.

'Why yes — Lunita Laredo. Now what became of her? I rather think she died or left Tweedy — left him more likely, as she was a bit of a fast one.'

'How did Major Tweedy meet her?'

'Major Tweedy — do you know I think that must be a bit of cod he was having. Sergeant-Major Tweedy might be more like it, for in his time here he had no such grand rank at all.'

'But how can that be? Wasn't he promoted from the ranks for his conduct at Plevna. I recall him telling us all about it.'

'Plevna! But good God man, there were no British regiments at Plevna at all. Tweedy was there as a volunteer fighting with the Turks against the Russians, a queer sort of thing to do when you think what butchers those barbarians really were.'

'This all surprises me. What else did they tell me? About the visit of General Grant. That must have happened?'

'Ah yes, let me see, about the end of 1878. A fine show. The old American consul was there, Honourable Horatio Sprague. But then everyone has heard of him by now.'

'How is that?' asked Bloom.

'Why, man, the *Mary Celeste*. He was the American consul when she was towed into harbour — he took a sensible line on the matter, not like Mr Solly Flood, who was convinced the crew were murdered by the men of the *Deo Gratias*. A strange business, but so is much of life. Living in a place like this, a no-man's-land between two countries, you feel as if you are on the borderland of the unknown all the time.'

Mr Bloom felt that his informant was about to slide away from the subject of Molly into a nether world of lost souls where he did not want to follow.

'That's all very interesting but I'm much more interested in the private lives of the people rather than in public events. Tell me more about the Major.'

The old man drifted back into the miasma of the past.

'Ah yes, Tweedy and Captain Groves were a pair of armchair generals. There was never a campaign but they didn't have the right way of it, the men in the field were wrong. Khartoum and Rorke's Drift — they would have saved the Welshmen and General Gordon. As well for them that the pair of them never set foot on a real battlefield, Verdun or Passchendaele, that would have shaken them up.'

'You'd have seen a lot of the Navy in those days.'

'The Navy? The British Navy, the French, the American, Russians, all of them on courtesy visits while passing so that we could admire their pretty paint work and their polished steel guns. Fear God and dreadnought! The ships had style in those days, handsome things and of course all the girls loved a sailor.'

157

Bloom's mind went back in time to the photograph of Lieutenant Mulvey in his dress uniform. He had been passing through Gibraltar on his way to the far eastern station, here today, gone tomorrow, leaving behind him the ineffable traces of a young girl's first real attachment. What had Molly seen in him, he mused. The attractions of that strong healthy body were obvious enough, but what had they shared aside from the animal delights of youth? Mere desultory chat under the shade of the park trees in the fierce summer sun? *Oh Poldy, the sailors were so nice.*

'But,' the old man resumed, 'it was Major Tweedy we were on about. I mind well now, for it is all coming back with a rush, that he was a Dubliner. Not I think a Dubliner like you, for he reminded me more of the officers from England than any of the soldiers from Ireland. You call him a major, but when he was here in the old days, he was little more than a drum major. He wouldn't be the first old soldier to promote himself to his true rank, giving himself the merit of unfought campaigns.'

'You surprise me,' said Bloom. 'He always seemed like a major to me.'

That hale and bluff boaster floated into memory, his end brought on by the whiskey: he drank himself sodden.

'What about Lunita Laredo, the woman he married?'

'Well frankly now that's all a long time ago.'

'I haven't come all this way to go home with nothing. Tell me. Whatever it is.'

'Well the Major, as we'll call him, came out here in 1860 or so. Gibraltar is not a favourite posting for the ranks. This is a small place, nothing to do, nowhere to go, beyond the houses down in Irishtown. He picked up in some way with this girl Lunita Laredo. Now I'm not saying she was not better than she ought to be. She was a peasant girl from over the lines, one of those villages up beyond Algodonales — later some said she should have come from Moron. Anyhow they set themselves up in a small house in Winter Port Street, without benefit of marriage, some said, though I don't think he could have lived out with her if that were the case.'

Bloom sat in silence.

'After a while the child came, the spit of the mother in

some ways but not in colour. The mother was dark and Moorish looking, a touch of the desert there. That was all well enough for a while. But there was too big a difference in age. The Major was besotted, but the girl, who was little more than sixteen when they married, got bored. One day he came home from the square and found she was gone. He thought she might have gone back to her village, but she hadn't, as he found when he chased her up. She had taken the train to Seville in fact. Years later after Tweedy had taken the child back to Dublin, we heard that Lunita had become the mistress of a colonel in the Spanish Army — the *Spanish* Army, merciful God — some monster of depravity that was cut to pieces by rebels in the Philippines around 1898. Someone heard he had been eaten by some wild niggers in the mountains but I don't suppose it is true. She must have been pushing fifty by then. She married a widower in Toledo who owned a wine shop. I suppose she must be dead by now. What would she be? Only seventy-seven though. Maybe not. If you are to meet your mother-in-law you'd better take the train north.'

Bloom felt washed out. It was all quite unexpected. He had not really thought about what he might find, but in his heart he had hoped for something more romantic. This was all so soundly real.

'Well I can't say that I'm not surprised. But thank you all the same. Odd in a way how character comes out in people. Her mother explains a good bit about poor Molly. About the only thing that stands is General Napier's brass bed.'

'Brass bed?'

'Yes. When Lord Napier left the Rock, old Tweedy bought his brass bed at the auction in 1883. Old Tweedy — or was it Molly — told me all about it. A bit of a distinction don't you know — a hero's bed and all that.'

Nulty looked puzzled for a moment. Then he laughed.

'Now I recall the brass bed. Lord Napier's did he say it was? That's good. That bed wasn't Napier's — that came from that Jew dealer, old Israel Cohen, down in Water Gate Street.'

He was invited to lunch but he declined. No, but he might come back before he left. He lunched by himself and as the heat of midday passed off, he made his way up the town

159

to the Alameda Gardens where he sat until the evening promenade began.

This place had been one of Molly's favourite memories of Gibraltar and he could see why. All the plants and green shady areas contrasted with the white houses below. There was peace up here, from the military bustle, the heat of the Levanter, from all thoughts of passion or recrimination. It was calm, peaceful and luxurious. Poor Molly, to have left all this, for dear, damp and dirty Dublin.

It was, he thought, time he was getting back.

1932

The Irish Sweepstakes. The Greatest Sweepstakes Ever Known. The Fairest Sweepstake in the World, Distribution to All Corners of the Globe. At the end of the Derby Sweep of 1931 over £3,500,000 had been distributed to thousands of lucky subscribers in all parts of the world.

The oldest Automobile firm in Ireland. Clement, Talbot, Lea, Francis, Hotchkiss, Mathis Cars. Cellulose Enamellings, Cylinder Grinding, Gear Cutting. S.T. Robinson, 33/34 South King Street, Dublin.

Fits Cured by Trench's Remedy. The Famous Home Treatment for Epilepsy and Fits and Nervous Disorders. Recommended by Clergymen of all denominations. Forty Years Success. Over 1,000 unsolicited Testimonials in one year. Convincing Testimony has been freely given by people in every walk of life.

My Farm's Not Big Enough for a Tractor — said the Old-Fashioned Farmer. The Fordson Tractor costs £140 at Works, Cork.

ROP Extra is the spirit for Speed — the last word in motor fuels. Russian Oil Products Ltd., 33 Lower O'Connell Street, Dublin.

Glorious New Church. Christ the King, Cabra, Dublin. Masses offered weekly for our benefactors. Donations gratefully received by John J. Flood, P.P., Arran Quay, Dublin.

Finola Lingerie — Silk and Art Silk Underwear made from the best materials by expert machine and hand workers. Made in Ireland by J.A. Gallagher Ltd., Lifford (Irish Free State) and Strabane (Northern Ireland).

KWR Radio Manufacturing Co. First manufacturers of Radio Apparatus in Irish Free State. 18 Clare Street.

Rathborne's Altar Wax Candles. Sactioned by the Hierarchy. Guaranteed and Stamped 75/-, 65/-, 25/-. Genuine Beeswax. Of Guaranteed Irish Manufacture.

To fashion Art that shall be Supreme, the Hand retains the Key. Gaeltacht Industries Limited. Everything Irish. *39 Nassau Street, Dublin, C.2.*

Bangkok — Calcutta — Vatican City — Schenectady — Toronto — Sydney — to mention only a few stations which can be received at Loudspeaker level on the Telefunken 32A. Price £19-10-0, complete with valves. Siemens Schuckert (Ireland) Ltd.

Cook and Heat by Electricity. More convenient, quicker, cleaner. Once you cook and heat by electricity you will wonder why you ever used any other method. There are no messy grates, no ashes, no dust or dirt with electricity. Just switch on — and leave the rest to the appropriate Ediswan Appliance.

13

The Last of Simon Dedalus

For some years Mr Bloom had lost track of, among many others, Simon Dedalus, the father of the poet who had amused Molly so many years ago.

Towards the end of 1932 he heard by chance that Simon (now an old man in his eighties) was ill in Drumcondra Hospital. He might not have long to live, as the old heart was giving him a lot of trouble. Mr Bloom hastened to see him.

The hospital was in Whitworth Road, overlooking the Royal Canal, near Glasnevin Cemetery, where the round tower memorial to Daniel O'Connell rose over all.

He found the old man propped up in bed with several large pillows behind him. He looked pale and thin, and at times his breathing came heavily. Simon reached out a long hand to greet him.

'It's great to see you,' Simon said weakly, but at once his spirits began to rally now he had someone to talk to.

'I heard you weren't so well, and it's only a step to come up here.'

'I'm only parked here until they find a place for me up the road.' He nodded in the direction of the cemetery.

'Ah now, Simon, you have a good time to go yet. How do they treat you here?'

'Very well indeed, considering what a cross old creature I am. I'm better off here than ever I was with the ungrateful brood of children I reared. Where are you these days? I was told you had left the daughter's place.'

'I have, but nothing disagreeable. I like being on my own, you know. I value the independence while I still have it. I'm lodging in Clonliffe Road, a very pleasant place with a widow named Quinn. I like being in a familiar piece of territory, don't you know. Not much of the city seems to stay as it was anymore.'

'Did it ever? I am afraid, Bloom my bucko, that you and me belong to another world. We are like those creatures they are always finding in China, missing links? No, living fossils! We are antediluvian!'

'I can't come out this direction myself without thinking back to before the Flood, as you might say, to Parnell's death. He seems to mean very little to anyone now what with republicans and socialists everywhere.'

'By God in those days there was more to a political cause than these riff-raff and gurriers,' Simon said with feeling.

'Ah Bloom,' he continued, 'Parnell, Parnell. What political interest I had myself was expended on the cause of Home Rule. I wonder if he had won in 1886 where we would be now?'

Just then a nurse appeared with a cup of tea for Mr Dedalus. Seeing Bloom, she returned with another cup — which was against the rules, but there was no harm in cosseting a couple of old men.

'That's grand, nurse. Thank you very much. I suppose we would have one of the Parnells in charge still. But tell me Simon, do you hear much from that son of yours, Stephen. Did he ever come back from abroad?'

'No he did not. I hear from him and the wife often enough, and he is always talking of coming back to visit me. The last time I heard of him he was having some difficulty about publishing some poems or stories. They blackguarded him over that business here in Dublin, but the book was published in the end, despite them. Queer stories they were too, not easy to read you know. Not the sort to have beside the bed when you can't sleep. I prefer Edgar Wallace myself.'

'He's married too, isn't he,' said Bloom, who recalled even as he spoke that there had been some scandal surrounding the departure of the Dedalus heir, and that the infuriated Simon had not forgiven him for years afterwards.

'He went away with a girl right enough, but it was a bit of time before he made an honest woman of her. Two children they have now, and a home in Paris. It was there he published that other big book of his — the name of it

164

escapes me at the moment – but there was a big row about that as well. We're all in it, I'm told.'

Bloom was genuinely surprised.

'We're in a book! I never heard that. What sort of a book? What does it say about us?'

Simon Dedalus grew vague.

'About the old days in Dublin when Stephen was young. Oh, it's supposed to be hot stuff right enough. Never read it myself. Banned here, I suppose. Like that Sean O'Faolain book there was all that row about. Did you know that his real name was Whelan and his father was an RIC man down in Cork city? A true bill. Didn't I have it from a cousin of mine who knew all about the family? There are clowns around now who'd tell you that a man like that was not Irish at all!'

Mr Dedalus, anxious not to end the visit, checked himself, recalling that his friend's right to call himself an Irishman had been questioned in the past. He remembered that old curmudgeon Cusack of the GAA disputing the title with Bloom on one memorable occasion in Barney Kiernan's.

Dubious claims to be Irish led inevitably to de Valera. 'I suppose if Dev gets his way, the Senate will be out on its ear. We are to have no more governors up in the Park either. After that bitter old foulmouth Healy it will be no loss. How anyone could elevate a creature like that after what he did to Parnell. Loyalty to the nation indeed!'

'If the Senate goes', said Bloom, 'it will be the end of a cosy seat for your man Mulligan. I can remember when he was Medical Mulligan, a notorious rake, not a fine elegant gent snipping out the tonsils of the rich and famous for fifty guineas a go!'

'A sound man though. Look at the way he escaped from those murderers in the troubles by pleading for a pee. And did you ever see that flying machine of his? A daredevil if ever there was one.'

Simon Dedalus always admired a sportsman, having been one in his own youth on the River Lee.

'Do you remember the first aeroplanes we saw in Ireland? When was it? August 1910, they had a display out at Leopardstown. Who was it flew that day – Captain Dixon, Cecil Grace and what was the name of the third?' asked Bloom.

'Diesel. No, Dexel. Wasn't that the same year that Robert Lorraine tried to fly across the channel from Holyhead and fell into the sea in front of the Baily Lighthouse?'

'Well I suppose Mulligan must be a daredevil,' said Bloom, going back on the conversation, 'with the things he says about de Valera his days are numbered in public life.'

'Do you know I haven't been about since Dev came in. Is it true they came in with pistols in their pockets?'

'Yes, it seems they feared a *coup d'état*. A bit foolish, if you ask me.'

'Tell me, Bloom, seeing that I've been stuck here all summer, what did you see of the Congress in June?'

The Eucharistic Congress held at the end of June had overshadowed all else that year.

'You missed a real event. I don't suppose the like of it would be seen again, unless it were a visit from the Pope.'

'I heard it over the wireless, of course, and it sounded wonderful. The nuns were mad with delight. But there were fellahs at the other end of the ward who only wanted to hear about the Tailteann Games.'

'We heard all the noise from Croke Park, but that had nothing on the Congress, what with the Papal legate and all.'

'I was thinking about him. What was the name of the Cardinal who came over in '04 for the opening of Armagh Cathedral?'

'That,' said Bloom with all the authority he could muster, 'was His Eminence Cardinal Vincent Vanutelli. I remember that well and the excitement it caused.'

'Did you go out to Dun Laoghaire to see the arrival?'

'I did not, nor did I swing one of the 14,000 invitations to the Garden Party in Blackrock. It was easier to get into the Viceroy's dos in the old days: I was at one of them.'

'Nor, I suppose to the opening in the Pro-Cathedral?'

'No indeed. But like the world and his wife I went to the Mass in the Park.'

'It's hard to imagine a million people standing together for Mass, even in the Phoenix Park.'

'Oh but it was some sight I tell you. And the enthusiasm. It says something for us, all the same, that we could organise an affair of that kind.'

'Even if Dev and his men wore soft hats instead of toppers,' said Simon with a laugh.

'Then the Pope spoke over the wireless. It was stunning, do you know. Just stunning. I'm not by way of being a religious person myself, but I was very moved. Then there was the procession out of the Park and down town for Benediction on O'Connell Bridge. Half a million walked, the papers said, and I can well believe it.'

'An historic occasion right enough, and wouldn't you know that Simon Dedalus would be stranded, high and dry in hospital. After so many years of trouble it makes a change to have a *religious* demonstration. The benefits will be with us for a long time.'

'Indeed they will, standing like guards along the Liffey bank. I mean those French affairs, those urinals. When everything else is forgotten, they will stand memorial to the raising of the nation's mind to God.'

The old men laughed. Then Simon said earnestly, 'I suppose in these hard times people are glad enough of the consolations of religion. We lost our moorings a long time ago.'

Mr Bloom recalled that Simon's wife had died young enough, in 1900 or thereabouts, and that there had been (how many was it now?) fifteen children. The old man in the bed before him was said to have drunk his way through his inheritance, his job and his pension. His was not a personal history unique in the annals of the nation. He had been a familiar figure in the city, had known all its secrets from his days in the Rates Office, and had recited them all in great detail.

'Swept away on the flood, antediluvian. I wonder why we bother, Bloom. Why do we marry? What has become of your daughter?' he enquired suddenly.

'She is married to a Corkman.'

'No people finer, if I don't say it myself, who will?'

'They have two children. A grand girl and a little boy. He's fourteen now. You can almost relive your life, like reincarnation, watching them grow. Their talk, their little ways, their walk even. A strange business. They would frighten you sometimes, were they not such interesting little creatures.'

Simon Dedalus reached over to his locker for a pocket book and fumbled in the crowded contents.

'Oh, here it is. A photograph of the family in Paris. A handsome crew.'

167

Mr Bloom held up the print to get the evening light on it: four people, a man and a woman in middle age, seated on a couch with two young people standing behind them. So this was Stephen Dedalus. He dimly recognised the features of the young poet in this bourgeois figure, so well dressed it was a shock by contrast with the shabby youth in canvas shoes he had once known. The wife appeared prosperous and satisfied. The children, however, had a haunted air. He guessed that behind that facade of ordinary, respectable life, there might well be a bit of turmoil.

Bloom left soon after, walking back along the Royal Canal and down towards the city. The long shadows of evening obscured the houses and gardens, much as the long shadows of history were closing on the lives of Simon and himself. In his young days, there had seemed to be so many people he knew about the place. Now they were all gone. Boylan had crossed to England in the Great War and gone into the theatre. Alf Bergan and Denis Breen, both dead. And Breen's wife Josie remarried. Even poor Nosey Flynn and Pisser Burke were gone. Lenehan gone over to Fleet Street, declined to take a job on the *Liverpool Post*. Mrs Sinico and Major Tweedy, taken by the drink. And John Henry Menton defending the undefendable during the troubles. The host of the dead was endless.

Soon after he heard that Simon Dedalus had died, but he never saw the notice in the paper and so he missed the funeral. He should have asked Simon what had become of their friends. He was told that Stephen Dedalus intended to put up a memorial to his father. Bloom thought that a plaque on one of the French urinals would be appropriate, but nothing came of the scheme in the end. Stephen had wanted a bench by the Liffey where other Dubliners could gossip as contentedly as his father had done. Nothing came of that either.

1936

A.G. Bruty, Contractor for Electric Lighting, Power, Bells, Telephones, etc., etc., no fee for consultation or estimate. 7 & 8 Eden Quay.

Belfast Household Linen Co. 28 Talbot Street, Dublin. Household Linen and Furnishings Specialists. Contractors to the Government, Hospitals and Hotels. Estimates Free.

M. Rowan & Co., The Seedsmen of Quality. Seed, Bulk and Plant Merchants, Farm and Garden Experts. Central City Branch, 1 & 2 Westmoreland Street, Dublin.

Tonge & Taggart, Windmill Lane, Sir John's Quay. Manufacturers of Iron Castings, Manhole Covers, and Cast Iron Tanks.

Don't Pay Income Tax — without Consulting Us. Repayments, Returns, Adjustments, etc., etc., MacDonagh & Boland Ltd., 51 Dame Street, Dublin.

Cattle Dealers and Salesmasters. Bergin, O'Connor & Co., Ltd. Livestock Salesmen. 11 St Joseph's Road, off Prussia Street, Dublin.

Grand Canal Company. The Grand Canal, with the system over which the company trades, serves 3 ports: Dublin, Waterford, and Limerick and 16 counties in the Irish Free State. The Cheapest and Best route for all kinds of merchandise. Regular services by Motor Barges.

14

All Change Here

As the years of his retirement crept on, Mr Bloom began to feel his age. In May 1936 he celebrated his seventieth birthday, in any man's life a notable day. At least in his sixties there was still something to look forward to. But in his seventies, he felt that time was running out.

And yet he remained hale and fit. To prevent himself brooding and so wasting away he had set himself a daily routine, which he followed as well as he could. He never let himself be prevented from some new lark if one came along, but generally he followed a predictable daily round.

His new lodgings, in a house in Clonliffe Road, were near his daughter, but with easy access to the city.

In the morning he would get up and dress with care. (He was always fastidious about his appearance.) Then he would join his landlady, the widowed Mrs Quinn, over breakfast. Mrs Quinn's other lodgers were all young students or civil servants, and were all away early with hardly anything to eat.

'Hardly worth catering for them,' she would moan, putting what they had left uneaten onto Mr Bloom's plate: bacon, eggs, kidney, sausage.

'It's a terrible shame, Mrs Quinn, a terrible shame. They don't appreciate a thing these young people, they have it too easy. Hard times I had in the old days, no breakfast at all sometimes. Pass it here. Thanks.'

In her long years of marriage Mrs Quinn (whose husband had managed a garage) had grown used to having a man in front of her for breakfast. As Mr Bloom with his old-fashioned manners had arrived soon after the death of Mr Quinn, he had slipped easily into his place, at the breakfast table at least.

So every morning Mr Bloom would descend to his place at the head of the table, receive his heaped plate of food and copies of the *Irish Independent, Irish Press* and *Irish Times*. The luxury of three papers was due to himself, his landlady (who admired Mr de Valera), and one of the lodgers who planned to be a freemason by the time he was thirty.

On this morning in June 1936, none of the papers made welcome reading. Mr de Valera's economic war was beginning to raise some doubts even in the mind of Mrs Quinn. She was much concerned by the sad fate of the slaughtered calves. The cooler views of the *Indo* were even less reassuring, and the foreign and imperial news carried in the *Irish Times* was always disquieting. Japan was again on the march: Mr Bloom was old enough to recall their victories against the Russians in 1904. Ethiopia brought back the recollection of Lord Napier. When was it he had stormed Magdala? He died in 1890, indeed, and, yes, that feat of arms had been in 1868. One advantage of being an old man, thought Mr Bloom: one always has a precedent for whatever is said to be new.

He sighed and put the papers down.

'Well Mrs Quinn, that was very satisfactory.'

'I am glad of that, Mr Bloom. And what will you be doing with yourself on a fine day like this?'

'Oh the usual round. Brisk walk into town, a little shopping, then on to the library. After lunch though, I am meeting the grandson and going out for a jaunt to the seaside.'

'Just the thing on a heavenly day like this. Will you take a packed lunch?'

'Thank you for the offer, Mrs Quinn, but no. I'm meeting the lad for a bit of lunch in the Bailey first.'

Taking the cardboard case in which he carried his notes and books, Mr Bloom left the house. He had been walking these city streets for seventy years — well, sixty-six — and he had not yet tired of them. For the man of varied curiosity there was always something to arouse the interest. His daily destination was the National Library in Kildare Street. To reach it, he would vary his route every day. Time was not strictly important, though he did like a good spell with his books.

Today he set off down Jones' Road, past the concrete

walls of Croke Park. Mr Bloom had never been curious enough to take himself within those walls, though the roars that greeted every score on Sunday afternoons were familiar to everyone in the neighbourhood. Still he supposed the rugby ground on Lansdowne Road was just as noisy.

Passing through Russell Street, he turned left down the North Circular Road and past that other great edifice of the district, the O'Connell's Schools in Richmond Street. Many a fine man got his grounding there — indeed it was said that in 1932 the change of government meant only the change of rule by Clongowes boys for O'Connell's boys. Probably true. Still, it was a tough place all the same, backing out onto that queer, blind street. The Christian Brothers had given the light of learning to many other poor, blind streets.

At Summerhill he crossed over the road, passed the church, and turned into Buckingham Street. Here he was passing along the edge of one of the most squalid districts of Dublin, where the wretched slums had once stood side by side with the plush brothels of Montgomery Street. Nowadays the Corporation was hard at work tearing it all down, and to remove the notoriety of the infamous 'Monto' had changed the street's name to Railway Street — a straight and narrow path. The girls had been given short shrift in the early days of the Free State by the combined forces of Mr Cosgrave and the Legion of Mary led by Mr Duff.

Mr Bloom passed on. He held no brief for the brothel owners and the girls themselves had had a hard time. He was only too glad that advancing age had relieved him of the burden of concupiscence. He had been down Monto only once, that night in the summer of 1904 when he had played the good Samaritan to the waylaid poet Stephen Dedalus. Never again, thank God.

He came out into the broader vistas of Amiens Street and saw by the railway station clock that he was making good time, as it was only half past nine. He turned round through Beresford Place, past the Custom House, a victim of the troubles like so much in the city, but now restored to business. This is where the cabman's shelter had been once — indeed had he and Stephen not gone there after their escape from the dangerous illusions of the brothel quarter?

By Butt Bridge he passed over into Tara Street, past Poolbeg Street (where Mulligan's exhaled the fetid odour of stale stout), the public baths where a queue already lined the pavement by the turnstile, and Townsend Street where the Coffee Palace was now a thing of the past. Turning left he went down Pearse Street, as they now called Great Brunswick Street, past the shop where the Pearse family had once had their monumental mason's business. The right trade they were in, Mr Bloom thought. Poor Willy, murdered merely for being his brother's brother. *Naked, I saw thee O beauty of beauty, and I blinded my eyes* . . . Sad business, right enough, but still with us, the Army Council and the Four Green Fields.

He turned up Westland Row, passing the post office which he had used as a *poste restante* address when he wrote to women. *Mr Henry Flower. Beauty of beauties.* Some beauty he'd got.

In Lincoln Place he turned into the chemists. The clean smell scented with the promise of healing greeted him.

'Good morning, have you any of that liniment I bought before. For the sciatica.'

'Ah yes. Mr Bloom isn't it? Yes indeed. Here we are. Will that be all? Two and six, please.'

The sciatica which troubled him was hereditary, from his father's family. He had taken to using the aconite liniment his father had used. One way out he supposed, when we grow too old for even our own comfort. Poor father. His anniversary was in ten days. He was in doubt as to whether he could get down to Ennis this year, as he had nearly every other year since his death in 1886. So long ago it was. Poor father, poor Athos. Poor mother too in her patient death.

Here at last, by ten o'clock, was the Kildare Street Club, with its mischievous monkeys climbing round the windows. They called it the last bastion of Anglo-Ireland, and nationally-minded people still related with relish how the members had attempted to get rid of Edward Martyn, when his labours for the new Ireland became more than they could stomach. Unable to because he was a long-standing member of the club, they sent him to Coventry instead. But Martyn had his own way, dining alone and saying his prayers in the reading room. A brave man; and had he not donated £10,000 to the Pro-Cathedral to fund the Palestrina Choir? No one made gestures like that nowadays.

174

At last he reached the narrow gate of the library and passed through. Going up the pillared steps, he passed through the foyer with its watchful sphinxes keeping their eyes on the readers, and up the stairs.

The library had changed a great deal since he had first known it. Not that he had used it much in the old days — the public library in Capel Street had been quite adequate for his supply of books. But he had been in and out a good deal during his stint on the *Freeman*. Lyster had been in charge then. Another man who gave much to the city and the country, but who was nearly forgotten. Who else was there? Richard Best, of course, that formidable authority on Celtic Ireland. He might have struck some as a dilettante when discussing mere English literature, but in Celtic Philology he had few rivals. And Robert Praeger too, the all-round man, naturalist, historian, archaeologist.

The library had opened to readers in 1890. For students at the university on the other side of Stephen's Green it had been an unofficial college library. Before the Great War, many men who were later to make their mark on Irish life could have been seen lounging about on the steps below, or bent over their books beneath the echoing dome.

But those had been the old days. Now that Mr Bloom was a regular reader, he had noticed how the library had fallen off after 1922. Foreign journals were no longer received. Magazines were cut off. For the most part, books themselves were bought only if of Irish interest. What had been growing into a great library was now starved of funds and falling back into the ranks of the second-rate. Mr Bloom knew where all the blame lay: next door with the legislators in Leinster House. Some of them hardly opened a book a year, he thought. The fruits of freedom indeed!

Mr Bloom filled up his slip and in a short time one of the attendants carried to his desk the green cloth-bound volume of *The Golden Bough* on which he was now engaged.

All his life, Mr Bloom had felt a great curiosity about religions, partly because of the patchwork of faiths that he himself represented. On retirement he thought he would take up again 'the religious question' which had so bothered him in his youth. What better way to approach the problem, he had thought, than to read his way through the formidable series of Sir James Frazer? As he went along he set out to look up the references which were quoted. These in their turn led to other books, other explorations. In this way, even though the library could not produce all he wanted, he had occupied himself for over five years. And still the end was not in sight.

Today, having less time than usual, he would be content to read through a section of Frazer, noting down as he went along the references to be searched out later. It was all quite enthralling and unproductive and suited him very nicely. The astonishing barbarities which Frazer discussed in his cool and unhurried manner made a contrast with the daily barbarities of the newspapers. He spoke of our debt to the savage: the savage was collecting the bill today.

Mr Bloom read on, until glancing up he noticed that it was now half past twelve. He was due to meet Rudy in the Bailey and must hurry. He returned his book, retrieved his slip and hastened down the stairs and into the street. Through Molesworth Street past the freemasons' chief lodge, which reminded Bloom that his own affiliation with that body was now defunct. The masons had once been a strong element in the business community of Dublin. His father had felt, and he had agreed with him, that it would do a young man of Jewish background, albeit connected to Protestantism, no harm if he had some power to help him on in life. The older firms had been permeated by the influence of the masons. The Knights of St Columbanus had been established to provide a Catholic organisation with similar weight. Mr Bloom had been a mason for some years, but when he became a Catholic on his marriage to Molly, it became difficult to maintain his membership. He had fallen away, but yet in rumour he had still been labelled a mason. This had caused him some difficulty with the Jesuits in Gardiner Street when Molly was in the choir there.

When he reached the Bailey it was already filling up. But there, with his lunch before him, was Rudy.

'I thought I would go ahead, grandpa. If you became absorbed you might well be late. Will you have something to drink?'

'A glass of burgundy, if you will, Rudy.'

176

Mr Bloom settled himself and surveyed the luncheon possibilities. He would have a long day before him. A chop he thought would do nicely. With food and drink sorted out, the two men relaxed.

'And how were your studies today, Rudy?'

'Well enough. The exams should not present too many problems. And your own? How are your researches into royal incest going?'

'Oh that was sometime ago. That and infibulation and female circumcision. Very strange. Only in my old age am I beginning to discover the real madness of the world. Truly terrible things are done in the name of sex.'

'You must come along one Saturday night and give the L and H the benefit of your researches and considered opinions. It would recall efforts like Brian O'Nolan's extempore on the perils of advertising.'

'I don't believe there is a forum in Ireland these days that would sit still while I talked.'

'Well, not sit still. They're a noisy lot.'

'They always were I believe. Still look at what they produced in their time. Tom Kettle, Sheehy Skeffington, Hugh Kennedy.'

'And in due course, yours truly.'

'Young puppy!'

Their plan for the afternoon was to make their way out to Dun Laoghaire or Sandycove and to have a swim and then to take themselves up to Dalkey. In Nassau Street they caught a Dalkey tram, which rattled them out past Merrion Square towards the sea.

'I see in the paper that Mrs Purefoy has had another baby in Holles Street. I must make time to call on her. Poor thing. Her mother-in-law also had a formidable number of children, poor woman. Wore her into the grave. The son, it seems, takes after the father. I think this is her fourth or fifth.'

'More terrible things done in the name of sex, grandpa.'

'Consider yourself lucky, young man. It's not everyone in this city would allow you to take such a light tone about the problem.'

The tram carried them down Mount Street, past Clanwilliam House, which always gave Mr Bloom a cold thought.

Well, such bloody battles were one way of reducing Mrs Purefoy's children. Another war — coming soon if we believed the papers — would show us how.

Ballsbridge with its large houses and the new premises of the Royal Dublin Society seemed like another world. Which it was: Pembroke township, not a noted haunt of nationalists. They had done away with its municipal independence in 1930 along with that of Rathmines. Central control seemed the order of the day. Curious how those who wanted freedom for themselves were never anxious for others to have it. Still, we would see. They said it would be a better way to administer a population of, what was it now, over 400,000. What a difference from his childhood, when it had been little more than half of that.

At Merrion Gates, the sea came in sight and it seemed that a large part of the city's population — or at least that part that was female and juvenile — was crowded onto the open swathe of sand that curved around the bay.

'As the tide is in,' said Rudy, 'I think we might as well go on to Sandycove and swim there.'

'The open beach or gentlemen only?' Mr Bloom asked.

'Oh the Forty Foot for me,' said Rudy.

The tram rattled on, through Blackrock, Monkstown, and Dun Laoghaire. They descended at Sandycove Road and walked down the gentle slope to the sea. Here too the houses suggested quiet withdrawn lives, lived outside of the hurly-burly of daily life in the new Ireland.

At this time of the day the little harbour was crowded, but in the Forty Foot itself, exclusively for men, there were only a few swimmers. *(Gentlemen Only — Bathing dress must be worn after 9 a.m.)*

As it was still a little too soon to swim after their lunch, they sat down on the rocks in the sun.

Above them on the brow of the point reared the solid bulk of the Martello tower, one of a series along the Dublin shore. Some of them were now sweet shops or tea-rooms, but this one stood empty. It had, Mr Bloom recalled, once been lived in, about 1904. The former senator Malachi Mulligan had held court there — the place had been written up in several books. A literary experiment of some kind it must have been, thought Mr Bloom. Cold in winter, though.

178

And now he thought of it, had Stephen Dedalus not had a hand in it as well?

He had taken a liking to that young poet. The father was a waster, and hardly saw what his son was. Bloom, however, having lost his own Rudy, valued a son. Stephen had qualities which would make themselves felt. Bloom had been attracted to him as a son. Molly too.

But now, here he was, with his own Rudy again. The young man stretched out at his ease in the sun reminded him of Stephen a little. A new generation had come. From what he heard from Rudy, the university once again had men of talent lounging about marbled halls. Rudy's father, like Simon Dedalus, hardly saw what was in his son. But his grandfather did. From his childhood Bloom had doted on the growing boy. He had developed into a handsome, striking young man of talent and intelligence. In him there lived the soul of little, long-lost, short-lived Rudy: metempsychosis.

'Well, what about that swim,' the young man said abruptly. The cold water in the shadow of the rock shocked the daydreams out of Mr Bloom and he emerged invigorated for the rest of the afternoon.

The plan was to go by the tram into Dalkey and to visit old Mrs O'Neill in her house at the top of Sorrento Road. This was one of those slowly rising roads that prove, at least for a man of seventy, quite breathtaking. The road ran along the railway, and once the Dublin train passed through the defile with a whistle, enveloped in a cloud of steam and smoke.

On the corner with Vico Road, Mr Bloom opened a wicket gate which led into a pretty garden, through stone steps mounted to a lawn before a little cottage. The door was answered by Mrs O'Neill herself.

'Poldy, how lovely to see you. And this must be your grandson. Come in, come in. On second thoughts, the kettle is just on the boil. We'll have a nice cup of tea. I'll bring it out into the garden.'

From this height they could look out over the curve of Killiney Bay down to Bray Head, and beyond that into the mountains of Wicklow. The beach between was as crowded as Sandymount had been.

179

'What a view, Mrs O'Neill. It quite astonishes me,' said Rudy, as Mrs O'Neill returned with the tea tray. She set this down on the bamboo table.

'If views were everything, I'd be a rich woman. Up here it's remote enough to my mind in winter. But that's a long way off in June. Let's enjoy what we have. Now, milk and sugar, or a little lemon perhaps?'

'Lemon for me,' said Mr Bloom. 'You're keeping well then?'

'I can't really complain, you know, Poldy. And how is your sciatica?'

'A twinge now and again, but a twinge only.'

'There seems to be a good crowd below,' said Rudy, as shouts of laughter reached them from the other side of the road.

'That's Sorrento Cottage — Mr Robinson's. Lennox Robinson, you know, of the Abbey. He puts on little plays in his garden now and again. Small boys are always hanging over the wall gawking at the actors. I believe they are only rehearsing today. A very nice woman his mother is, but he's, you know, very artistic. Drinks like a fish.'

They were like that at the Abbey, thought Mr Bloom, remembering Yeats tottering down Nassau Street from Hanna's with *Riders of the Purple Sage* and *Trouble at the Bar-B* tucked under his arm. *George, George, call the Sheriff.* Dreamers, or hard as nails. As the man in charge, Bloom imagined that Robinson must be as hard as nails.

'Rudy here is planning on going to the Abbey tonight, to see *Hassan*. I don't suppose you would care for such a play?'

'Oh no thank you, Poldy. I never venture far in the evenings these days. I'm not an adventurer like you.'

'Indeed a short holiday in Gibraltar doesn't make me an adventurer, nothing like the things that befall those who take the Golden Road to Samarkand.'

'A strange play for the Abbey surely,' said Mrs O'Neill. 'I thought it was only Irish plays they put on. Is there no romance to be got out of our own streets and our own lives?'

'Romance seems out of place anywhere these days,' said Bloom. 'The spirit of the age is realistic. It has to be, I

180

suppose. What happens on ordinary streets tends to be very sordid stuff, better kept off the stages of this fair country.'

After Rudy had left, the old couple sat on in the lengthening light of evening, silently watching the pink clouds tumbling down the horizon.

'Why is it that sunsets always remind me of my youth?' said Bloom, at last.

'Perhaps because they are fading away like your memories.'

'Ah, some memories never fade.'

'Get away with you.'

'Ah no, Josie, I still recall the old Christmas of 1888, sitting out with you on the couch under the stairs, and Molly coming upon us all in a rage.'

'Ah Poldy, why did you marry her?'

'Why did you marry Breen and then O'Neill? Once bitten, you should have been twice shy.'

'The company. You grow used to a man, even if he does wear his boots in bed. God, men can be dreadful things.'

She smiled at him, and Leopold recalled that smile as it had been half a century before. Dear dead days beyond recall. Love's old sweet song. The scent of lilac, of hot candle wax, the rustle of silk on polished parquet, the whish of a fan. The houses still stood, if he could find them in what were then remote suburbs, and which still were remote, if only in his mind. But the people, that way of life, which had seemed so calm and settled and continuous, the generations of peace before the Great War, yellow silk reflected on polished silver, all gone now. As he watched, he saw again the cold stars on the night they drove down from Glencree.

'She was unfaithful to me you know. At least three men, maybe more, dozens I sometimes imagined. Her nature, I suppose, needed more than I could give. But she stayed with me. When I was small I thought I was ugly. She said I wasn't and she loved me. Told me she loved me on Howth Head. I remember.'

'Oh Poldy, don't dwell on it all.'

'I don't dwell on it. I dwell in it. When I lie in bed at night — I don't sleep too well these days and Charles Morgan is not always enough to send me off. I think about it and it all floods back, shapes, sounds, tastes. Overwhelms me. But Molly, she was much more than I could ever know. Secrets she had, must have told you, never revealed to me. But then all the secrets of my youth she never knew.'

There was silence. From below faint echoes of laughter mocked the loneliness of their lives.

'Look,' said Josie Powell, as he always thought of her, 'that one star has come out. What is it they call that one?'

'Hesperus,' said Bloom, and he felt the cold of night along his back.

1937

The Payne School of Dance and Mime. 50 Middle Abbey Street, Dublin. Director: Miss Sara Payne. Irish Dancing under the direction of Mr. George W. Leonard. The only school where the student can study the Classical Ballet side by side with the National Irish Dance Tradition, with the definite aim of achieving a new and Irish Choreography.

Kennedy's Bread. Finest Quality Made. Well Baked. Full Weight. Excellent Flavour. Purchasers are requested to see that the name "Peter Kennedy" is stamped on each loaf.

Churchman's No. 1. New Map of Ireland Cards for Gifts. A coloured map of Ireland in sections forms the new series of cards being issued in all packings of Churchman's No. 1 Virginia Cigarettes. All the former valuable gifts together with new additions are available in exchange for complete sets of Map Cards, which are numbered for the convenience of smokers and are each of the same value. 10 for 7d. 20 for 1/2.

G & T Crampton Ltd., Builders and Contractors, Hammersmith Works, Ballsbridge, Dublin. Telegrams: 'Foundation, Dublin'.

Barry's Tea post free in four pound parcels anywhere in Ireland. Blends at 1/8; 2/2; 2/6; 2/10 and 3/2. Awarded the Empire Cup at Grocers' Exhibition, London, 1934.

Pictures and Picture Framing in good taste. The Victor Waddington Galleries, 28 South Anne Street and 19 Nassau Street, Dublin, C.2.

15

Closing Time

His last landlady, Mrs Quinn, had considered Mr Bloom quite unremarkable. Interesting, yes. And good company. But not remarkable, not in the way (for instance) that the notorious Bird Flanagan was remarkable. It was hard to imagine Mr Bloom becoming part of the city's folklore.

When people talked of Dublin characters, they always lamented their passing. There were no 'artists' as in the old days. Mr Bloom was not an artist in that class at all. His life passed uneventfully, and his character and temperament were of a kind that hardly made him memorable outside his own circle. But Mr Bloom had class. There was no doubt about that. Among the Dubliners of his generation, mild and unassuming as he was, he had class.

All his life Bloom had moved at a tangent to those around him. By race he was a Jew, in a country where Jews were a small minority, nearly all newly arrived. Anti-semitism had never bulked large in Ireland, but it did exist, even if it was only at the level of jokes about the 'vandering vindy vendor'. He had been reared as a Protestant; though his grasp of that religion was weak enough, as his father had lapsed back into the faith of his fathers. Leopold Bloom had no faith. When he married Molly he converted to Catholicism, but that did not mean much to him either: it was just a means to an end. Indeed as he grew older himself he became more interested in religion, hence his researches (such as they were) into its origin and development. Such studies were likely to have left him with no feelings at all on religion, merely opinions.

Race and religion had become important labels in Ireland after Parnell. Irish and Catholic were synonymous at an instinctive level for Irish nationalists. So all his life Bloom was also at a tangent with Irish politics. Certainly he espoused, in his youth, the ideals of land reform and Home Rule put forward by Davitt and Parnell. But the revolutionary violence of the Fenian tradition, the surgical knife syndrome in Irish life, that he could not follow. While the enthusiasm of militant Irish nationalism rose around him, Mr Bloom by intellectual outlook and temperament moved further away from his countrymen. If he was anything at all, he was at heart a philosophical anarchist. But at any one time they are a rare breed in Ireland.

The real Bloom, then, was not an historical person, so to speak, but a sensational one, a man who lived for his thoughts and feelings.

He felt pity and sympathy for everything, from the cat he would feed in the morning to some lame dog of a poet picked up on his way home at night. But his sympathy extended also to the animals in the cattle market, to women and their problem about public facilities, to starving children and doddering old women. This sympathy grew out of instinctive respect for life rather than from any scrupulously reasoned intellectual position.

As a consequence he always had some respect for others. He could even find some forgiveness for Hugh Boylan who had trespassed more than somewhat on his good nature. But he would also be careful not to disturb others, not to intrude on privacy; he found coarse jokes disgusting in most company.

Not indeed that he did not have a low opinion of many other Dubliners. There was a type of loud mouthed boor he actually disliked. But the ordinary run of people, such as Reuben Dodd and Nosey Flynn and Bantam Lyons, were merely dirty, foolish or stupid.

One cannot go through life liking everyone. Nevertheless for much of his life Bloom was a sociable creature, ready with hospitality, a smile or a warm word for the hardworking or hard pressed. He would make a habit of repressing his hasty anger — least said, soonest mended, after all.

These sympathies and feelings found their deepest expression in his family. What he felt for the memory of his old father, and his unfortunate mother, for Molly in all their difficulties, for Milly and the lost Rudy, and now for his grandson, these were feelings for what Burke would have called 'our small platoon' from which all larger social feelings arise. It was all too easy, especially in Ireland, and especially in the early twentieth century, to declaim a ringing love of the people and kick one's old wife about on a Saturday night. While Bloom had his family, the world beyond could wait.

The squalid he now found repulsive, just as once he had sought it out for sexual satisfaction. Now he was more fastidious. He was in the habit of bathing regularly — this at the turn of the century in Dublin was a rare thing to do, and would have astonished many of his fellow Dubliners. The city was not called 'dear dirty Dublin' for nothing. But Bloom found nothing delightful in dirt. He would see that his trousers were pressed and changed daily, that his jacket was brushed and his hat reblocked. Rumpled stockings, dirty hands or chins dripping food disgusted him. He was himself so ordered and neat that the one occasion on which he went to Drimmies without his tie remained forever a memorable day.

Nevertheless he had a quick eye, and was not above seeking out something sensational. By now, his sexual drive had waned, and though he would admire a girl in her new finery, the lust of his earlier years no longer troubled him. Indeed as his life advanced the melancholic side of his character became dominant. He was bathed in an almost oriental inertia. It was this which had prevented him from 'improving his position' when he might well have, from going into the advertising business for instance, when everyone said what a natural talent he had for the trade.

These black moods would come upon him, when he would feel an overwhelming sense of lassitude. The world spinning through the endless night of the universe, our days an illusion caused by the rotation of the earth. He would feel his personality almost drift away from him, as if he were someone else, as if no-one were anything at all, as if nothing were everything, and everything nothing. Perhaps he should have been a monk, he had often felt in later years. And yet he had no faith in God; when he was younger, he would not have given up the pleasures of life for the privations of prayer.

It was as well perhaps that he could laugh at himself and

his antics now and again. He had always been amused at the innocent notions of 'silly Milly', and had relished Molly's earthy wit. He was always struck by the incongruity of words and notions: 'Chamber music', for instance seemed to him to have unsounded possibilities. To survive all those jobs he had needed his sense of humour.

There were other aspects of his taste in music, art and literature. He was interested in words and philosophical speculations of a shallow kind. His taste in books ran to the sensational, in art to the rude. The poets and writers of the much vaunted revival in Ireland meant little to him. Yeats was nice enough, down by the Sally Gardens only. And Colum had a nice thing, She Moved through the Fair. But George Russell and that esoteric nonsense and absurd vegetable eating was quite ludicrous. If he wanted a good read he would turn to Conan Doyle rather than Shan Bullock.

But it was music that had always seemed most important to Bloom. In old age, he had realised that he owed this lifelong interest to his mother. At one time she had passed almost completely out of his memory, as his father occupied his thoughts. Now he found, as his recollection of recent events became vague, that his childhood was returning to him with exceptional vividness. This was not unusual in old men. But he found that lying half-asleep in his chair of an evening, his mind would flow back over the past.

Mrs Quinn one evening had left him some small tarts for his evening tea. Taking one up he noticed that they were made of almond paste and biting into it he felt the sharp tang of the raspberry jam underneath, the soft crumbling texture of the pastry. These were (how it all came back) just as his mother had made them. He could see her now, standing in the back kitchen of the house in Clanbrassil Street, a shining white apron about her, rolling out the pastry and warning him to keep his fingers out of the jam or there would be none to go in the tarts. The blacked kitchen range warmed the room, and outside the snow lay thickly over the garden grass. What year was that? 1872? Yes the year the trams came, the Pillar to Rathmines or Terenure for a penny. Or was it the winter before, when the Gaiety opened and St Stephen's Day became set aside for pantomime? He held his mother's hand tightly and thrilled to the adventures of Sinbad the Sailor.

His mother introduced him to music, playing the upright piano brought from Piggots in the front parlour. Her green dress and white lace shawl, her long hands on the ivory keys, her lovely voice.

He had forgotten what a lovely voice she had. Enchanting it now seemed, soft and melancholy in tone. Poor mother, was she ill even then? Her hectic cheeks and pale complexion gave the hint that she was. Nodding in his chair the music flowed around him, carrying him off into a sleep.

> Just a song at twilight, when the lights are low
> And the flick'ring shadows softly come and go.
> Tho' the heart be weary, sad the day and long,
> Still to us at twilight comes
> Love's old song, comes love's old sweet song.

A hand shook his shoulder.

'Your tea, Mr Bloom! It'll be cold.'

'Oh thank you. Yes, I was drifting away there for a moment.'

... At the End of the Day

When it came, the end was sudden.

By 1937 the city was creeping out into the countryside. Those new estates which had been built to rehouse the 'real Dubliners', the people of the city centre, were already being built, often over green fields familiar to the courting couples of an earlier generation. New roads ran out among them, with new names, now redolent of the new Ireland, Mellowes Road rather than Wellington Place.

The old canals still held the city in a circle, and had to be broken through. So it was that work was begun by the Corporation in 1936 to rebuild and enlarge the bridge over the Grand Canal at Clanbrassil Street. When completed the bridge was to be opened with suitable ceremony on Sunday, 31 January 1937, by the lord mayor of Dublin, Alderman Alfred Byrne, TD.

Alfie Byrne was a character from another era, who had lingered over into the idealistic days of Mr de Valera. A census taken on 26 April 1936 had shown that the population of Dublin (now enlarged to include the old townships of Pembroke and Rathmines) was then 467,691. Mr Bloom and Alfie Byrne could both remember a time when it had been only 304,778, and when the city had been a pleasanter place.

While the country bled to death, and people streamed aboard the emigrant boats, Dublin swelled like a great wen. Having grown by over a third, Mr Bloom now felt it was no longer the Dublin he had known: it now belonged to 160,000 strangers like his son-in-law. But Alfrie Byrne, however, going back to the old days before the Great War, belonged to a fashion Mr Bloom could still admire. He was a handsome figure, in his old fashioned suit and his silver watch chain

191

looped over his waistcoat. If he, Bloom, had ever achieved his dream of being Alderman Leopold Bloom, MP, JP, Knight of St John of Malta, he would like to have been a figure like Alfie Byrne.

From 1923 on Dublin had been without a lord mayor, so that the return to local democracy in 1930 and the election of Alfie Byrne had been something of a landmark. For three terms he had presided over Dublin in his genial style. (On 28 June 1939 he was replaced by Mrs Tom Clarke, the relict of the martyred patriot of 1916, a woman who could not be said to exude the same easy bonhommie.)

So when it was announced in the papers that the lord mayor of Dublin would be officially opening Emmet Bridge over the canal at Clanbrassil Street, Mr Bloom thought this was an occasion he should not miss, even though he was not as steady on his legs at the age of seventy as he would have wished to be.

He set off early in the morning, planning to walk to the scene along roads familiar from childhood, stopping somewhere for lunch in a public house and so back home again in the evening.

The South Circular had, he found, become much busier, the houses just a shade shabbier, since the evenings of the 1880s which he passed wandering there in the gloaming with his friends, setting the world to rights, expounding philosophical novelties with all the confidence of the callow and inexperienced. He could laugh at it now, but not too much. It had been a brighter day for all that when he was twenty-one, and a longer evening too.

After his lunch, he turned down Bloomfield Avenue and into Windsor Terrace to reach the new bridge. He planned it this way to save until afterwards a look at the house in Clanbrassil Street itself in which he had been born.

The street was quite crowded, and when the mayor and his party made their appearance, there were loud cheers and familiar greetings, which Mr Byrne acknowledged in his accustomed way.

The bridge was duly blessed by the local parish priest. Then the lord mayor made a speech, extolling the bridge's fine qualities as an example of the reconstruction of their city which would help to keep Dublin what they all knew

192

it to be beneath its often shabby appearance, the seventh city in Christendom. Loud cheers. Ah yes, thought Mr Bloom, Alfie Byrne had style.

The seventh city in Christendom. He looked down from the new ferroconcrete ballustrade over the sluggish waters of the Grand Canal, along which came the steady chugging of a canal barge, which passed under the bridge and off into the distance. Mr Bloom followed it in his mind. Through green and lush Kildare, it went past St James' Wells from where the Guinness Brewery drew its water — stout being made, contrary to legend, not from Liffey water but canal water. And then out into the bleak brown water of the Bog of Allen, to Tullamore (a place no one claimed to come from, he had once been told) and out into the Shannon river, into the deep dark lakes, where the storm clouds came down in the evenings like some stage set for the twilight of the gods. And further west his father lay buried. The thought made him cold. It was time to be going home.

He left the bridge and crossed the road to reach Clanbrassil Street, passing the little shop and the narrow side alleys choked with families. Such names they had, Costello's Cottages, for instance, you would wonder what their history had been. Then the houses fell back behind front gardens, with lawns and flower beds. This was the terrace and here was number fifty-two, 'the house where I was born/the little window where the sun came peeping in at morn.' This at least, he realised with surprise, had remained untouched. He lingered and looked over the road to the later houses on the other side, trying to recall the names of the neighbours. Yes, Joyce he remembered. The low winter sun, now setting down behind the roofs, dazzled him and as he inadvertently stepped off the pavement into the road, the world turned and collapsed into darkness. For a moment he thought this is only an accident.

But it was fate. The Ford car managed only to brake for a moment before it hit the old man staggering from the kerb. There was no blood, but the creature was hardly conscious. A small crowd gathered, commenting on the disaster. Who was he? No one knew. Not from round here anyway. He looks Jewish, perhaps he's from one of those streets on the other side of the Circular Road. An ambulance came, and wrapped in a grey wool blanket, the body was lifted inside.

It was only a short way to the Meath Hospital. Mr Bloom was still barely alive when he was admitted there at ten minutes past five. He regained enough consciousness to murmur something indistinct to the nurse, then lapsed again into silence. He died at twenty-five minutes past six. He was seventy years old.

From his pockets they took the following items: a packet of letters addressed to Henry Flower, a pension book in the name of Leopold Bloom, a photograph of a well-built lady in Victorian evening dress inscribed *Molly Glencree 1895,* a set of keys with an ornamental keyring *A Souvenir of Gibraltar*, the wrapped remains of a sandwich and a piece of potato.

By some oversight no notice of his death was put in the papers. Only a few friends attended the funeral in Glasnevin the day after. Coming away afterwards his son-in-law remarked to Milly: 'I thought as much. For all his old chat about knowing this one and knowing that one, few enough came to his funeral. Dublin people are queer. You soon forget people in a big city.'

And soon enough Mr Bloom was completely forgotten, hardly remembered even by his daughter Milly. Only his grandson, occasionally pausing to admire some novel scene on the city streets, felt a pang of longing to share it with the old man.

Index

195

Eccles Street, 76, 84, 99
Ellis, Mrs, 12
Ennis, 26ff, 40, 174
Erin's King (boat), 65
Eucharistic Congress, 166ff

films, 108, 146
Flower, Henry, 95ff, 174, 194
Frazer, Sir J.G., 175
Freeman's Journal, 39, 42, 76ff, 83, 128, 132, 136, 141, 175
Freemasons, 2, 36, 43, 84, 90, 141, 172, 176

Gaiety theatre, 42, 46, 115, 188
Gallaher, Mrs Joe, 39
Gardner, Stanley G., 71ff, 105
George V, 116
Gibraltar, 33, 58, 151ff, 194
Gladstone, W.E., 25, 40
Glencree, charity dinner at, 57ff, 181, 194
Goldberg, Owen, 15, 18, 25, 143
Golden Bough, The (Frazer), 175
Gonne, Maud, 71, 77
Goodwin, Prof., 44
Great War, the, 121ff
greyhound racing, 142
Griffith, Arthur, 77ff, 127, 134ff, 141
Gunn, Michael, 25, 45ff, 69, 115

Hainau, Freiherr von Hauptmann, 10
Harcourt Street, 45, *see also* High School
Hardwicke Street, 114
Harrington, Tim, 43
Hassan (Flecker), 180
Hegarty, Fanny (later Higgins), 10
Hely's, 37, 63, 65
Higgins, Ellen (later Bloom), 10, 12, 23, 27, 188
High School, 13–18, 45, 133, 143
Holles Street, 63ff, 99, 100
Home Rule, 25, 33, 40, 43, 88, 116, 134, 164, 186
Hooper, Alderman John, 37, 42
Howth Head, 36
Hughes, John, 66, 148
Hungary, 9, 77ff, 134

Irish Homestead, 106
Irish Independent, 141
Irish National Invincibles, 24
Irish Republican Army, 127, 129, 133
Irish Times, 76, 90

Jesuits, 89
Jews: in Hungary, 9; in Ireland, 11, 26, 37, 43, 113ff, 143, 185

Karoly, Julius (later Higgins), 10
Kellet's, 23, 25
Kelly, Bridie, 18
Kiernan's, *see* Barney Kiernan's
Kossuth, Lajos, 10, 78

Laredo, Lunita, 33, 36, 152, 156, 158ff
Larkin, James, 118ff
Leeson Park, 23, 98
Lenehan, a journalist, 57ff, 168
Linwood (house), 37, 83
Lombard Street West, 43, 44
Lyons, Bantam, 115, 186

MacBride, John, 71, 77
McCarthy, J.F., 2, 113ff, 121ff, 130ff, 135, 138
McCarthy, Rudy, 124, 142, 176ff, 194
McCormack, John, 105, 145
Mallow, concert at, 56
Menton, John Henry, 32, 37, 113, 168
Modder River, battle of, 70, 133
Mooney, Mrs, 114
Mulligan, Malachi, 165, 178
Mulligan's, 55, 174
Mullingar, 87, 101ff
Mulvey, Harry, 59, 72, 152, 154
Murphy, William Martin, 43, 119, 141
Mutoscope, 99
Myriorama, 14, 32

Napier, Lord, 159, 172
National Library of Ireland, 77, 175
New Ireland Assurance Co., 141
Nulty, Michael, 154ff

O'Dowd, Elizabeth, 53, 56
O'Driscoll, Mary, 68
O'Faolain, Sean, 165
Ontario Terrace, 68
O'Shea, Captain William, 39
O'Shea, Katharine (later Mrs C.S. Parnell), 39, 54

Palme, wreck of, 95

196